Exploring Canada

MANITOBA

Titles in the Exploring Canada series include:

Alberta

British Columbia

Ontario

Quebec

Yukon Territory

Exploring Canada

MANITOBA

by Gordon D. Laws and Lauren M. Laws

LUCENT
BOOKS®

THOMSON
⁕
™
GALE

San Diego • Detroit • New York • San Francisco • Cleveland • New Haven, Conn. • Waterville, Maine • London • Munich

THOMSON

GALE

Development, management, design, and composition by Pre-Press Company, Inc.

LIBRARY OF CONGRESS CATALOGING-IN-PUBLICATION DATA

Laws, Gordon D.
  Manitoba / by Gordon Laws and Lauren Laws.
    p. cm. -- (Exploring Canada Series)
Summary: Examines the history, geography, climate, industries, people, and culture of one of the most diverse of Canada's provinces.
Includes bibliographical references and index.
  ISBN 1-59018-047-X (lib. bdg. : alk. paper)
  1. Manitoba--Juvenile literature. [1. Manitoba. 2. Canada.] I. Laws, Lauren M. II Title. III Series.
  F1062.4 .L39 2003
  971.27--dc21
                                                2002014364

Printed in the United States of America

Contents

Foreword

A ny truly accurate portrait of Canada would have to be painted in sharp contrasts, for this is a long-inhabited but only recently settled land. It is a vast and expansive region peopled by a predominantly urban population. Canada is also a nation of natives and immigrants that, as its Prime Minister Lester Pearson remarked in the late 1960s, has "not yet found a Canadian soul except in time of war." Perhaps it is in these very contrasts that this elusive national identity is waiting to be found.

Canada as an inhabited place is among the oldest in the Western Hemisphere, having accepted prehistoric migrants more than eleven thousand years ago after they crossed a land bridge where the Bering Strait now separates Alaska from Siberia. Canada is also the site of the New World's earliest European settlement, L'Anse aux Meadows on the northern tip of Newfoundland Island. A band of Vikings lived there briefly some five hundred years before Columbus reached the West Indies in 1492.

Yet as a nation Canada is still a relative youngster on the world scene. It gained its independence almost a century after the American Revolution and half a century after the wave of nationalist uprisings in South America. Canada did not include Newfoundland until 1949 and could not amend its own constitution without approval from the British Parliament until 1982. "The Sleeping Giant," as Canada is sometimes known, came within a whisker of losing a province in 1995, when the people of Quebec narrowly voted down an independence referendum. In 1999 Canada carved out a new territory, Nunavut, which has a population equal to that of Key West, Florida, spread over an area the size of Alaska and California combined.

As the second largest country in the world (after Russia), the land itself is also famously diverse. British Columbia's "Pocket Desert" near the town of Osoyoos is the northernmost desert in North America. A few hundred miles away, in Alberta's Banff National Park, one can walk on the Columbia Icefields, the largest nonpolar icecap in the world. In parts of Manitoba and the Yukon glacially created sand dunes creep slowly across the landscape. Quebec and Ontario have so many lakes in the boundless north that tens of thousands remain unnamed.

One can only marvel at a place where the contrasts range from the profound (the first medical use of insulin) to the mundane (the invention of Trivial Pursuit); the sublime (the poetry of Ontario-born Robertson Davies) to the ridiculous (the comic antics of Ontario-born Jim Carrey); the British (ever-so-quaint Victoria) to the French (Montreal, the world's second-largest French-speaking city); and the environmental (Greenpeace was founded in Vancouver) to the industrial (refuse from nickel mining near Sudbury, Ontario left a landscape so barren that American astronauts used it to train for their moon walks).

Given these contrasts and conflicts, can this national experiment known as Canada survive? Or to put it another way, what is it that unites as Canadians the elderly Inuit woman selling native crafts in the Yukon; the millionaire businessman-turned-restaurateur recently emigrated from Hong Kong to Vancouver; the mixed-French (Métis) teenager living in a rural settlement in Manitoba; the cosmopolitan French-speaking professor of archeology in Quebec City; and the raw-boned Nova Scotia fisherman struggling to make a living? These are questions only Canadians can answer, and perhaps will have to face for many decades.

A true portrait of Canada can't, therefore, be provided by a brief essay, any more than a snapshot captures the entire life of a centenarian. But the Exploring Canada series can offer an illuminating overview of individual provinces and territories. Each book smartly summarizes an area's geography, history, arts and culture, daily life, and contemporary issues. Read individually or as a series, they show that what Canadians undeniably have in common is a shared heritage as people who came, whether in past millennia or last year, to a land with a difficult climate and a challenging geography, yet somehow survived and worked with one another to form a vibrant whole.

A Diverse People Looking Forward

Manitoba is notable for the striking contrasts among its residents, landforms, and weather. The people who now intermingle and, at times, conflict with each other share a remarkable history of adapting to an often-harsh environment. Culturally, Manitoba is the most diverse province in Canada, with native tribes ("First Nations"), the Métis (French for "mixed," these are descendants of native-European unions), European immigrants, and people with African, Asian, and other heritages all being represented. Even among Europeans and other white settlers, the differences are notable—Manitoba's immigrants have come from Scotland, England, Ireland, Germany, and Italy as well as from Iceland, Russia, and the United States. These diverse cultures' distinct religions, customs, and heritages built the foundation of the modern province.

The establishment of Manitoba as a province also illustrates its distinctly multi-ethnic character. A Métis rebellion sparked Manitoba's acceptance as Canada's fifth province in 1870, three years after the original four (Quebec, Ontario, New Brunswick, and Nova Scotia) joined together as the new nation of Canada. Led by Louis Riel, a fiery figure who remains controversial in Canada today, the Métis defied the attempts of Canadian officials to ignore what the Métis' referred to as their nation. This original province was only one-eighteenth of Manitoba's current size (its small, rectangular shape lent it the name "the postage stamp province"), and it didn't last long as a homeland exclusively for the Métis. Yet many Métis remain in Manitoba today, and they are still fighting for land and rights that they say have been unjustly denied.

"The Narrows of the Great Spirit"

The name Manitoba is another indication of the province's roots in its early heritage. The name is taken from the Cree words *Manitou bou,* which mean "the narrows of the Great Spirit." The phrase refers to Lake Manitoba, whose narrow center is only one-half mile (one kilometer) wide. Waves hitting rocks on the northern shore make a bell-like, wailing sound that aboriginals said came from a great drum beaten by the spirit Manitou.

Implied in the province's name is a deep aboriginal connection to the land. Indeed, most inhabitants are somehow

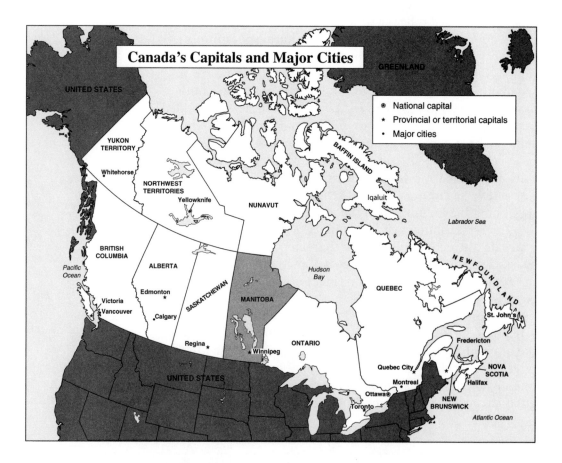

■ *First Nation and Métis men paddle a canoe wearing their traditional dress.*

rooted to the land. The land itself is indicative of the province's differences, with landforms varying widely across the province and people's lifestyles differing accordingly. The province's northernmost shores of the Hudson Bay feature virtually uninhabited, treeless tundra. In the parklands and lake regions of the southeast, Manitoba offers picturesque rolling hills and sandy beaches lined with vacation homes.

Much of the central part of the province is covered with boreal (northern) forest. Only a few roads penetrate this vast wilderness, dotted with a handful of native reserves (reservations) and small towns dependent upon the logging, mining, or hydroelectric industries. Within the past decade the province has also taken dramatic steps to protect more of its old-growth forests and wilderness lands, more than doubling the acreage set aside in provincial parks. Of course, such actions often trigger bitter disputes. These occur not only between environmentalists and proponents of development but between Manitoba's earliest peoples (who claim their land was taken unfairly from them) and property owners, including individuals, companies, and the provincial government.

Where Winnipeg Is King

The contrasts in the province extend, as well, to the striking differences between city and rural life. Winnipeg is the population center of the province. Its metropolitan area numbers almost 700,000 people and accounts for three in every five of Manitoba's residents. The next largest city, Brandon, houses only 40,000 people. The Winnipeg metro area is Canada's eighth largest, and the city plays a dominant role in provincial life. Winnipeg is home to some of Canada's oldest and most renowned cultural institutions, including fine universities, museums, ballet and symphony orchestra companies, and art galleries. The city itself is a melting pot of diversity. Aboriginal peoples often come to the city seeking jobs. The unique French quarter in St. Boniface blends European and Métis French heritage, and immigrants from all over the world are congregated in other sections of the city.

West of Winnipeg are tall grass prairies and fertile plains that have become prime farming land, mostly growing grain but also field and hay crops. The Assiniboine River, which

■ *A 1939 photograph of the Royal Bank (left) and City Hall in downtown Winnipeg, Manitoba.*

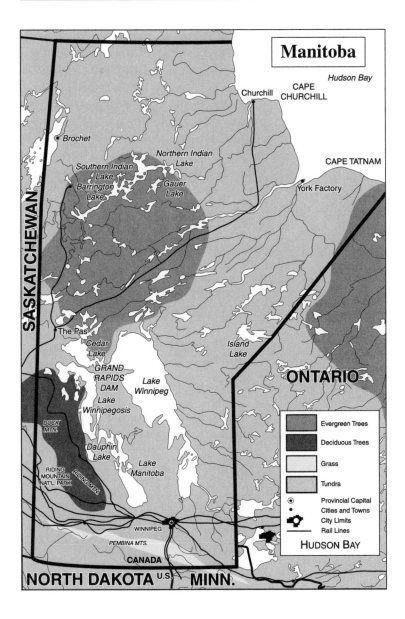

flows into the province from the west, and the Red River, which enters from the south, intersect at Winnipeg. They were major trade waterways in past centuries and a number of early fur trade forts were built on their banks. The rivers' regular flooding helped provide the soil that now supports agriculture. But the flooding became increasingly a problem by the mid-twentieth century, as suburbs of Winnipeg and farm communities were sited in the flood plains. The province has had to devote substantial amounts of money in recent years to major public works aimed at controlling the flow of the Assiniboine and Red Rivers.

Manitoba's population is crowded into a relatively small segment of the province. If you drew a line diagonally across the province, from the town of Flin Flon on the Saskatchewan border to Lake of the Woods in Manitoba's southeast corner, some 95 percent of the province's residents would be included in the triangle. That leaves approximately 60,000 residents spread throughout the central and northern expanses that make up almost four-fifths of the province's land.

An Uncertain Future

Today, Manitoba's diverse population faces an uncertain future. The province and the Winnipeg metro area are growing only very slowly, both in terms of population and economic opportunity. A century ago, the province flourished as a national power. Its location at the edge of the prairies made it a key shipping and transportation center for grain, lumber, and other products. The opening of the Panama Canal in 1914, however, made it much cheaper to ship goods east and west by ships. The province then suffered through a long period of labor problems, high rates of unemployment, and political discord.

Even today, the province has not regained its previous stature as a national power, though its cultural and natural resources are considerable. For example, the province possesses more hydroelectric potential than its sister prairie provinces, Saskatchewan and Alberta, but can develop it only by respecting conflicting viewpoints related to land claims and environmental issues. How Manitoba's disparate groups sort out their differences on such questions will present the central challenge to the province as it attempts to establish itself more firmly as an economic and political power within Canada.

From the Prairies to the Bay

C entered in Canada, Manitoba is often lumped together with Saskatchewan and Alberta as one of the
prairie provinces. In reality, less than one-fifth of
Manitoba's land is prairie. With approximately half of the
land forested, and lakes and rivers abundant throughout the
province, Manitoba is rich in natural history. The central and
northern parts of Manitoba, where the underlying Canadian
Shield (a continent-sized band of ancient rock) sweeps across
the province, offer rich mineral deposits. The province also
encompasses large stretches of marshy, poorly drained lowlands in the far north. The only prairie province bordering
the Hudson Bay, Manitoba has land that supports hognose
snakes in the south and polar bears in the north. The contrasts between the land types are striking, and even within the
supposedly uniform prairies, the land varies in elevation, soil,
and vegetation. Manitoba's scant population of slightly more
than one million people means that much of the land, particularly in the north, remains pristine.

Tall Grass and Rolling Plains

The prairies and parklands of southern Manitoba are the
province's most hospitable region, with many of those people
who live outside the Winnipeg metro area congregated in the
trade corridor that follows the Trans-Canada Highway toward
Regina in neighboring Saskatchewan. Most plains areas are
covered with mixed grass—medium-length grass of different
varieties—but a 40-mile-wide (65-kilometer) band of land
west of Winnipeg is classified as tall grass prairie.

■ *Portions of Manitoba's rugged landscape are located along the coastline of the Hudson Bay on the province's northern border.*

Travelers often complain that the prairie provinces are flat and uniform, but such is not the case in Manitoba. Historian Gerald Friesen, in describing the land stretching from Manitoba westward, says, "Even a century of cultivation cannot conceal the fact that the region is dotted with tree-clad hills and valleys. They interrupt the miles of rolling plains, sometimes as low blue ranges on the horizon, sometimes as winding slashes cut deep into the surface of the land."[1]

The land of today's province was once covered by glaciers that began to recede more than twelve thousand years ago toward Hudson Bay. As they did, they carved the valleys, formed the hills, and deposited the soils that make up today's plains. In all, about one-third of Manitoba consists of the so-called interior plains, the biggest section of which is the Manitoba lowland.

The Manitoba lowland encompasses the Red River valley and much of the area surrounding the province's three huge lakes, Winnipeg, Winnipegosis, and Manitoba. It ranges from 600 to 900 feet (185 to 275 meters) in elevation. In glacial times, the vast Lake Agassiz covered the lowland. When most of the lake dried, it left behind land that ranges from sand dunes to rich soil. Because the area is so low-lying, with rivers draining into it from the east, west, and south, it is particularly vulnerable to flooding. Even so, much of Manitoba's best farmland is in the Red River valley and the lowland plains, where the dark soil yields plentiful crops of wheat, barley, vegetables, oats, and various oil seeds. In the Pembina valley south of Winnipeg and to the west of the Red River, hill slopes include stands of aspen, oak, and birch trees that create a parklands area.

In the southwestern corner of the province, the lowlands give way to a "second prairie level" or western upland that rises about two thousand feet (six hundred meters) above sea level. This area is separated from the lowlands by the Manitoba Escarpment, a lengthy geological feature that runs in a northwestern direction from south of Fargo, North Dakota, to beyond the northwestern shores of Lake Winnipegosis. The terraced ridges and steep cliffs of the Manitoba Escarpment (also known in the United States as the Pembina Escarpment) were formed as the western edge of ancient Lake Agassiz. The

■ *A lone oak tree stands amongst a sea of grass in Manitoba's prairie region.*

■ Facing Nature in Winnipeg

Winnipeg residents have learned to poke fun at themselves, in large part because of their city's geography and climate. Residents have given the city several nicknames: "Winterpeg" for the icy winter months, "Windypeg" for the winds that sweep off nearby Lake Winnipeg, and "Waterpeg" for the spring floods that in the past have turned downtown streets into waterways. Another popular joke relates to how flat the area is: "It's so flat that if you let your horse out of the barn, you can still see him running three days later!"

There is no denying that Winnipeg can be brutally cold. The city experiences an average daily low of −6° F (−21° C) in January, making it the largest city in the world with such cold winter weather, surpassing even cities like Moscow, Helsinki, and Oslo, which are located at more northern latitudes. The frequent high winds in Winnipeg rival those of "Windy City" Chicago and have been known to blow over trucks and turn stop signs into deadly missiles. The good news is that the sun shines despite the brutal cold and gusty wind—Winnipeg averages some four hours of sunshine per day from December through February.

Winnipeg can't do much about the cold and wind, but it has applied an effective technological fix to the flood problem. Located at the junction of

escarpment is responsible for some of Manitoba's most striking landscapes, including deep gorges and Baldy Mountain, the highest point in the province at 2,730 feet (832 meters). Large parts of the escarpment lie within environmentally protected areas including Riding Mountain National Park and Duck Mountain Provincial Park.

Wildlife of the Plains

The mixed-grass prairies, parklands, and lakes of southern Manitoba provide ideal habitat for a range of wildlife. Birds like the orchard oriole, the lake sparrow, and the indigo bunting favor open areas near rivers and marshes. Forested areas along the Red River and its tributaries are also good spots to find various species of deer, moose, grouse, and wild turkeys. In addition, the open southern prairies between forestlands are home to a variety of animals, including coyotes, badgers, and foxes. A small herd of plains bison (buffalo) the Red and Assiniboine Rivers, Winnipeg has experienced a number of devastating floods due to the combination of flat terrain and heavy rain. One of the most disastrous floods in Canadian history was the Red River Flood that occurred in the spring of 1950. The Red River crested at thirty feet (nine meters) above normal near Winnipeg, leading to the evacuation of one hundred thousand people, one drowning, damage to five thousand homes and buildings, and $550 million in property losses. This disaster prompted city and provincial officials to obtain partial federal funding for an extensive flood control plan. By 1969 the finished system was in place, including dikes on the Red River, the Shellmouth Dam and Reservoir on the Assiniboine at the Manitoba/Saskatchewan border, and floodway channels capable of partial rerouting of both the Red and Assiniboine Rivers. The system faced its biggest test in 1997 when Winnipeg was hit with "the flood of the century"—water flow in the Red River was even greater than in 1950. Yet the flood control system worked. Some dikes needed emergency reinforcements, and twenty-eight thousand residents along the Red River had to be temporarily evacuated, but downtown Winnipeg stayed dry.

roam in Riding Mountain National Park. In sand marsh areas east and southeast of Winnipeg, where willows, sedges, and mosses cover much of the moist soil near rivers, various owl species live as well as deer and moose.

In the lake region around Lake Winnipeg and Lake Winnipegosis, many of the sandy wetland areas provide excellent habitats for frogs, snakes, and turtles. Among the birds frequently seen are Canada geese, common loons, great blue herons, western meadowlarks, and great egrets. Plant species include saskatoon (a berry-producing shrub of the rose family), chokeberries, and bog birches. In higher elevations around the lakes, aspen are common, and white spruce, balsam poplars, and jack pines can be found. Forest and marshlands provide good cover for moose, deer, black bears, and muskrats.

When Manitoba decided to designate a provincial bird in the mid-1980s, the most popular choice was one of the world's largest owls, the great gray. It is a spectacular bird with a five-foot wingspan that usually lives in remote areas but can

■ *The majestic great gray owl is Manitoba's provincial bird.*

fairly often be spotted near roads and towns in Manitoba. It feeds on mice, rabbits, and voles and nests in abandoned hawk or raven nests. "A bird of mystery," notes biologist Robert Nero, "the great gray owl bears in its aloofness some of the remoteness of the vast northland; its plumage the color of lichens and weathered wood; its soft hooting, part of the wind."[2]

The Manitoba Shield Area

The striking diversity of the plains gives way to even greater land changes moving north. The ice sheets that receded from present-day Manitoba thousands of years ago had profound effects on this central part of the province, which is typical of areas dominated by the Canadian Shield. A great rock foundation stretching across much of northern Canada, the shield is crystalline and granite rock scoured by receding glaciers. Most of the small amount of soil on the shield is affected to one degree or another by permafrost, permanently frozen ground that has trapped water and frozen it solid, thus preventing deep-rooted plants and trees from growing. The foundation underlying the permafrost is made up of intensely compressed rock that was twisted and turned millions of years ago. Most of the topical features were stripped away from the surface by the receding glaciers, leaving mostly flat, open land.

The small, rounded hills that remain and the intermittently frozen soil also affect the land features across the north. Because shield areas are poorly drained, there are numerous shallow lakes and small, turbulent rivers. Maps of Manitoba show the northern shield area checkered with small groupings of lakes and rivers, and these areas are surrounded by marshes and bogs that make overland travel virtually impossible. Further south, just north of the three major lakes, the land is heavily forested.

In the northeastern corner of Manitoba, at the edge of the shield, lie the Hudson Bay lowlands. The region is not actually part of the Canadian Shield—it is a low plain of sedimentary rock rather than granite and crystalline rock—but like the shield, it is marked by general flatness with small, rounded hills. Much of this area is spongy, bog-like ground called muskeg. Small patches of stunted coniferous trees mark this area.

Though challenging to live on, the Canadian Shield provides some valuable natural resources for the province. The hard-rock shield yields nickel, ore, copper, and other precious metals, and stretches of it in the central part of the province are heavily forested. Still, less than 10 percent of Manitoba's population lives in the shield area. Of that population, nearly 60 percent is of aboriginal descent, many of whom live on lands once occupied by their ancestors. The town of The Pas, located 350 miles (550 kilometers) northwest of Winnipeg, is a major population center of the forested central region, and it is home to only some fifteen thousand people. Thompson, located further north in the center of the province, is a Canadian Shield mining center of roughly the same size. Other towns, most built around mining or logging, are much smaller. Native reserves also cater to mining, hunting and trapping, or tourism. Many of these isolated aboriginal reserves and towns are reachable only by air because of the difficulty of building roads in marshy, lake-strewn, and perma-frosted areas.

Manitoba Shield Wildlife

Much as the land contrasts sharply with the southern plains, so too does the shield wildlife contrast sharply with plains wildlife. The permafrost and severe weather of the north diminish typical plant life, preventing common grasses and mild-weather trees and animals. Even so, many species of plants, animals, and other life-forms have managed to survive.

The area surrounding and including the Hudson Bay lowlands is a key wildlife study area—and no wonder. Stands of spruce are mixed in with marshes, ponds, and peat bogs, providing habitats for rare varieties of plants and animals. Both subarctic and boreal plant species survive here. The area is a key

■ *Lynx are just one of the many animals that call the Hudson Bay lowlands home.*

nesting ground for prairie Canada geese who come north to hatch eggs. More than 225 other bird species have also been identified in the region. Otters and beavers can be spotted in rivers. In addition, the area provides a home for lynx, arctic fox, and wolverines.

The most northern part of Manitoba's Hudson Bay coastal area is tundra, the "polar desert" characterized by few trees, abundant rock outcrops, and low annual precipitation. Arctic and subarctic species of grasses, mosses, lichens, and sedges survive here. Late spring brings a colorful smattering of flowering plants like the purple saxifrage. A few animals, including the polar bear and coastal caribou, are well adapted to the mostly barren tundra. Beluga whales return to the estuary of the Churchill River each summer from elsewhere in the Hudson Bay to give birth and feed their young. Polar bears' main prey, seals, can also be spotted in the cold coastal waters. Birds such as golden eagles and trumpeter swans arrive in the summer and migrate south for the winter.

In general, Manitoba's northernmost regions remain untouched and little explored. The forbidding climate and poorly drained soils make the area unsuitable for agriculture. Only the hardiest of Manitoba's residents care to live here, and they often do so at the expense of regular contact with others. Still, there is raw beauty to be found, a thread that is common to the other key landforms of the province.

A Province of Trees

Forests are scattered throughout much of Manitoba. The most expansive stretches, however, include the boreal forest of northern Manitoba and the mixed-wood forest of central Manitoba. Both forests are vital ecosystems for numerous species, and they are important for Manitoba's logging and forestry industry.

The boreal forest grows mostly across the upper central portions of the province where the land is just blending into the Canadian Shield. It comprises mostly coniferous, or cone-bearing trees, including white and black spruce, balsam firs, and jack pine. Like shield transition forest areas even further to the north, the boreal forest provides habitats for muskrats, beavers, and wolves. But loggers also cut the forest, and it provides a significant economic boost to towns like Flin Flon on the western border. As a result, disputes between loggers and environmentalists over Manitoba's forests are common.

Spruce, pine, and other coniferous trees also grow in the mixed-wood forest just to the south of the boreal forest. The various deciduous trees in the mixed-wood forest include Manitoba maple, white birch, poplar, and aspen. In addition to being a home to numerous bird and plant species, the

■ Polar Bear Capital of the World

The northern port city of Churchill on the Hudson Bay has identified a unique tourist attraction in recent years: polar bears. In October and November of each year, hundreds of polar bears gather along the shores of Hudson Bay, waiting for the water to freeze so that they can begin hunting seals. For fees between $2,000 and $4,000, adventure companies take tourists on expeditions into the heart of polar bear country. Tourists ride in huge tundra buggies, specially designed vehicles with viewing platforms as well as indoor toilet facilities. The buggies' large, underinflated tractor tires tread lightly on the raw tundra earth and keep travelers high off the ground and away from curious bears.

In Churchill, polar bears have been known to wander into club meetings, restaurants, and homes in search of leftover scraps of food. They appear almost harmless, with friendly faces and warm fur coats. Even though Churchill polar bears seem to be at ease with people, viewers are warned to stay clear of the animals—they can be deadly when threatened or when they are too hungry. Thankfully, this has been rare: polar bears have mauled to death only two Churchill residents in the last hundred years, despite numerous encounters.

mixed-wood forest is an important habitat for large animals like the black bear, woodland caribou, and elk. As with the boreal forest, the mixed-wood forest is coveted by loggers for its profitable trees such as old-growth aspen, and environmentalists often actively oppose logging.

The Rivers and Lakes

In addition to its large forests, Manitoba is unique for the sheer acreage of water left behind when the last ice sheet receded. Like the forests, Manitoba's lakes and rivers provide striking natural splendor, habitats for many species, and an economic boon for residents.

■ The Prairie Provinces' Only Port

The northeastern edge of Manitoba borders the Hudson Bay, and tiny Churchill is home to the only port of the prairie provinces. The port became a true shipping venue in 1931 with the arrival of the railroad from The Pas. The railroad made it possible to transport grain across the province for shipment to eastern Canada and beyond. To this day, no road comes within 150 miles (240 kilometers) of Churchill. The main advantage to shipping grain from Churchill to Europe, rather than from Montreal to Europe, is that the trip by sea is some one thousand miles (sixteen hundred kilometers) shorter from Churchill. By avoiding the locks and canals of the Great Lakes and the St. Lawrence Seaway, ships to and from Churchill can also save time and money.

Churchill has one major drawback as a port: it has a prime shipping season of only July to November, when the Hudson Bay is ice free. Shipping companies can use the services of icebreaking ships during other months, but this requires costly insurance policies. Churchill can pray for global warming, but it has also taken a number of other steps in recent years to increase its attractiveness as a port. It has added increased train unloading capacity to transfer grain, using its 140,000-ton grain elevator, from railcars to ships. With federal and provincial funding, it has dredged the Churchill River estuary to allow access for larger, deep-sea tankers. Some 90 percent of its port volume is accounted for by grain, but Churchill is now also shipping minerals, lumber, and manufactured products to Europe, Russia, the Middle East, and Africa.

Lake Winnipeg is the largest lake in Manitoba and the sixth-largest freshwater lake in Canada. With an area of more than 9,400 square miles (24,400 square kilometers) and a length of some 260 miles (420 kilometers), the lake is larger than the state of Vermont and is Manitoba's most prominent natural feature. Lake Winnipeg is Manitoba's largest remnant of Lake Agassiz, the great glacial lake that covered much of the province at one time. Lake Winnipeg receives water from the Red, Winnipeg, and Saskatchewan Rivers, and the Nelson River drains it to Hudson Bay. It is home to numerous varieties of trout, carp, bullhead, and other fish that are either native to the waters or stocked. Commercial and sport fishermen make a living from the lake, while the area also supports a large tourism industry, including summer resorts on the shores. The other most prominent large bodies of water in Manitoba are Lake Winnipegosis and Lake Manitoba.

Of equal or greater importance to Manitoba's ecology and economy are its rivers. The Red River of the southern prairies is perhaps the best known of Manitoba's rivers. Running some 550 miles (900 kilometers) long, it flows south to north and empties into Lake Winnipeg. The Red is home to many varieties of fish, most prominently the channel catfish, a large bottom-feeding fish prized by fishing enthusiasts. More important, the river and its largest tributary,

■ *The Nelson River, one of Manitoba's many rivers, drains water from Lake Winnipeg to the Hudson Bay.*

the Assiniboine River, provide water to the rich farmland of the Red River valley.

Despite its location in the remote north, the Churchill River, like the Red River, has not escaped human tinkering. In the 1960s the provincial public power utility, Manitoba Hydro, decided to save money by not building any dams on the Churchill but rather diverting much of its water to the Nelson River, some 100 miles (160 kilometers) south, where a number of generating stations were being built. In 1977 engineers completed the diversion channel, which takes Churchill River water out of Southern Indian Lake and through the Rat and

■ Hydro Development in the North

Since the early 1900s, government energy planners have looked at Manitoba's turbulent northern rivers as prime spots to locate hydroelectric plants. The rivers' many stretches where water moves rapidly, over falls or through narrow passes, make them ideal for power generation. At the top of the planners' wish list was the Nelson River, which runs from the northern end of Lake Winnipeg to the Hudson Bay. The first generating station on the Nelson was built in 1960 to supply power to mining and smelting operations in Thompson. But planners were particularly interested in exploiting the river's energy farther south, where power could most cheaply be directed to the bulk of Manitoba's residents.

Tapping the power potential of the northern rivers became more urgent by the 1950s, when the Winnipeg River, which drains into the southern end of Lake Winnipeg, was completely developed for its hydroelectric potential. Rapidly growing Winnipeg needed more electric power. A 1963 agreement between the government of Manitoba and the government of Canada secured the financing needed to install transmission lines from north to south and begin construction on generating stations. In 1974, five First Nations groups began consulting with Manitoba Hydro and the government to regulate flood control along the river. In November 1974, the Kettle Generating Station on the Nelson River was completed. The 1,272-megawatt generating station was the province's largest at the time.

Later, diverting water from the Churchill to the Nelson River increased generating power in some spots up to 40 percent of the Nelson's capability alone. Finally, channels and dams were constructed on Lake Winnipeg to increase the water outflow in the winter months, when water tends to flow more gradually. The increased flow guarantees steady power generation year-round. Today Manitoba derives 95 percent of its electricity from waterpower.

Burntwood Rivers to the Nelson. An average of 60 percent of the Churchill's natural flow into the Hudson Bay is diverted to the Nelson River. This draining of the Churchill River remains controversial because of potentially adverse effects on fish and waterfowl.

The few lakes and rivers just described represent only a tiny fraction of Manitoba's incredible reservoir of freshwater, which ranges from tiny, almost uncharted rivers to lakes that are among the largest on the continent.

■ *Polar bears are a tourist attraction for the city of Churchill. The bears frequently wander into the town in search of food.*

The Climate

One aspect of Manitoba's unique character is the severity of its climate. In January, daily lows in the north average −18° F (−28° C), and the temperature in Churchill may sink to −45° F (−45° C). Churchill has snow on the ground from October to April. Storms originating in the Hudson Bay can cause hurricane-force winds to sweep across northern Manitoba. Winters are cold across the province, but even in the south, spells of below-zero windchill can cause frostbite to unprotected skin in a matter of minutes.

Manitoba winters are notorious, but the province does generally enjoy four distinct seasons, with summers in the lake region being especially pleasant. In Winnipeg, average daily highs from May to September stay within the mild range of 64° to 78° F (18° to 26° C). In the north, temperatures average a mild 54° F (12° C) in mid-summer, with a high of 96° F (36° C) recorded.

Yearly rain and snowfall are light, and the amounts decrease moving west and north. The Red River valley receives slightly more than twenty inches (fifty-six centimeters) per year, while the western border gets about eighteen inches (forty-six centimeters) per year. In the far north, only about fifteen inches (thirty-eight centimeters) falls.

Diverse Contrasts

Manitoba's landscape is often breathtaking, whether in the deep forests or the rolling plains. Even though relatively little rain or snow falls, the land is dominated by water. Large and small lakes occupy much of the land, and rivers cut through valleys in other parts. The people required to manage such contrasts are diverse. Over time, the people who have come to the province have used the land in different ways, exploiting its animals for fur but eventually shifting to agriculture, mining, and forestry.

The First Nations, the Europeans, and the Métis

M anitoba's early history was dominated by the indigenous First Nations, the Europeans who established the fur trade, and the Métis peoples that resulted from the mingling of the two. When European explorers first entered Manitoba, they were seeking the elusive Northwest Passage, the northern sea route that would open trade across the top of the continent. They found First Nations peoples who had been established in the land for millennia. The volatile relationships among natives and diverse groups of newcomers were characterized by rivalry, competition, uneasy cooperation, and, frequently, violence.

The First Nations

Today, more than sixty First Nations groups claim parts of Manitoba land as their ancestral inheritance, giving a hint at the diverse aboriginal population Europeans first encountered. The aboriginal populations were made up of complex societies with social structures and hunting and migrating patterns that they had honed for centuries. While many aboriginal groups existed, two of the most numerous and important at the time of the European arrival were the Chipewyan and the Cree.

The Chipewyan lived on the Canadian Shield in areas stretching from present-day Quebec to the area of the Great Slave Lake. In the area of present-day Manitoba, they inhabited the northern

■ *The Chipewyan were nomadic and became important fur traders.*

Hudson Bay lowlands. Unlike more rigidly organized tribes, like the Cree, the Chipewyan lived in small bands of primarily extended family. They spoke an Athapaskan-rooted language and were nomadic, hunting the caribou and following them in their seasonal movements. They were rivals of the Wood land Cree who occupied the central areas. The Cree dominated the aboriginal fur trade with the Europeans and generally drove the Chipewyan to the northern areas. Nevertheless, the Chipewyan became important northern fur trading partners with the Europeans as explorers moved into the central and northern portions of Manitoba.

The Cree were one of the most diverse and widely spread tribes in Manitoba and in Canada. The Cree in Manitoba originated south of the Churchill River near the Chipewyan land. Many, however, did not remain in the area, choosing to follow the development of trade as it gradually switched from woodland beaver to plains buffalo. Such followers came to be known as the Plains Cree. Those who did not venture so far south but settled in the forests and river areas of central present-day Manitoba came to be known as the Woodland Cree. Still others remained in the marshy lowlands of the Shield where they hunted, trapped, and later traded with European settlers.

The broad reach of the Cree across present-day Manitoba (and across Canada) is testimony to the power of the Cree Nation. The Cree were fierce warriors, driving the Chipewyan and other less powerful tribes from the central plains and woodland areas. The Cree, like the Chipewyan, lived in close-knit family units, but in the spring and summer, they gathered in bands as large as one thousand or more to renew relationships and participate in ceremonies and festivities. The Cree hunted and trapped both for game and for trade between them and other bands. They likely originated the method of hunting buffalo by stampeding the animals into enclosures where they could be killed in numbers. Enterprising and resourceful, the Cree grew in power, compared to other tribes during the years after the arrival of the Europeans. The Cree became key European guides, leading the French and later the English on expeditions north and west to trade.

Eventually, the economic benefits Europeans brought to the First Nations paled in comparison to the diseases such as smallpox that the Europeans also brought along. First Nations peoples would eventually suffer devastating losses and near extinction, culminating in their signing treaties with the Canadian government that gave the tribes only remote and isolated reserves of land in exchange for resource development rights.

The Fur-Trading Europeans

The cutthroat competition and the violence that marks much of Manitoba's early history are rooted in the fur trade. What evolved into a bloody rivalry between the two great fur-trading

■ The Assiniboine of Lake Winnipeg

The Assiniboine are generally credited with being among the first people encountered by Europeans in present-day southern Manitoba. A branch of the Yanktonai Dakota of the upper United States region, the Assiniboine moved north and west to the Lake Winnipeg area before the seventeenth century. Eventually, they spread out around the lake, and bands settled along the upper Saskatchewan and upper Missouri rivers. They spoke a language similar to the Sioux in the United States.

Like many other plains First Nations groups, they had no permanent villages. Rather, they lived in family-oriented bands that migrated with the buffalo and other game animals. After Europeans arrived, the Assiniboine traded readily and partnered with the Europeans in expanding the fur trade. From this, they received guns and horses, which increased their ability to hunt buffalo and other game. They generally allied themselves with the Cree and were enemies of the Blackfoot.

Like other First Nations, the Assiniboine were ravaged by disease, particularly smallpox, in the early nineteenth century. In 1874, their numbers decimated and the buffalo nearly extinct, they joined the Cree in signing Treaty 4 with the Canadian government. Today, more than five thousand Assiniboine live in the northern United States, and about two thousand are scattered across the prairie provinces of Manitoba, Saskatchewan, and Alberta.

companies of the time, the Hudson's Bay Company and the North West Company, was compounded by a rivalry between the two great European powers of the 1600s—France and England. Eventually, the English, and later the Hudson's Bay Company would prevail, but the divide between French and English in Manitoba began with the arrival of Europeans.

The first European to set foot in present-day Manitoba was Sir Thomas Button, an English captain and navigator who had been sent to find the missing Henry Hudson and explore the huge bay named after the explorer. (Mutinous crew set Hudson, his son, and seven others adrift in a small open boat in what was later named the James Bay in 1611; their bodies were never found.) Button landed at the mouth of a great river on the Hudson Bay in 1612. He named the river for a ship's master, Robert Nelson, who died there.

Over the next seventy years a number of explorers searched the shoreline of the Hudson Bay for the Northwest Passage. Thomas James's voyage of 1631–1632 went down the west coast of the Hudson Bay into the bay on its end, a huge body of water in its own right that was named after James. British and French explorers also began to approach the area of present-day Manitoba from the east as they sought to establish trade routes and forts for the fur business. The French explorers

■ *The Hudson's Bay Company, an English fur-trading company, established trading posts throughout the Hudson Bay region. Pembina Post, seen here, was located in Manitoba.*

Pierre-Esprit Radisson and Médard Chouart des Groseilliers in 1659–1660 explored the shores of Lake Superior and told of an area rich with furs. Their report failed to inspire much response from the French king, but King Charles II of England was eager to expand British influence in the area.

In 1670 King Charles established the Hudson's Bay Company with a charter that granted the company all the land drained by the Hudson Bay. This was an immense spread of land (almost 500,000 square miles, or 1,250,000 square kilometers), much bigger than thought at the time. It came to be known as Rupert's Land, named after the king's first cousin and the administrator of the land, and it included much of present-day Manitoba. Shortly after its inception, the Company began to explore the region. In 1684 it built a trading post, York Factory, on the Nelson River on the other side of a small peninsula from the Hayes River. The Hudson's Bay Company lost control of York Factory to French forces or fur traders a number of times over the next two decades as Britain and France battled for supremacy in Europe and in North America. The British ultimately prevailed, and the French signing of the Treaty of Utrecht in 1713 returned all Hudson Bay drainage land to Britain and compensated the Hudson's Bay Company for losses. The site of York Factory was moved in 1715 to the mouth of the Hayes River, which became a major riverway for the fur trade. (The Nelson is a larger river but has many areas of fast rapids, making it more dangerous for canoe travel.) York Factory became the Hudson's Bay Company's most important trading post for more than a century, and it remains Manitoba's oldest permanent settlement.

Despite the Treaty of Utrecht, the French remained enterprising rivals of the British for dominance in the fur trade in the early eighteenth century, especially in the area to the west of Lake Superior. Among the most renowned French explorers were Pierre La Vérendrye, his sons, and a nephew. Originally a soldier and then a farmer, La Vérendrye answered the lure of frontier adventure in his early forties, moving to the north shore of Lake Superior. In 1731 he convinced the French minister, Jean Maurepas, to grant him a three-year monopoly on the fur trade in the area. Maurepas over the next ten years continually prompted La Vérendrye and his sons to explore and expand their trade westward. They successfully did both, building up the fur trade of New France,

■ Henry Kelsey's Journey from York Factory

In the late 1600s, the Hudson's Bay Company did not aggressively pursue exploration and settlement inland from Hudson Bay, but it did try to expand its trade. In 1690, the Company dispatched young Henry Kelsey on a mission to bring back native peoples willing to deal in furs at Hudson Bay.

Much of Kelsey's journey is wrapped in myth (his journal is vague on many key issues), and few hard facts are known about him. Yet his journey remains remarkable. From York Factory on the west coast of Hudson Bay, he traveled with a party of Indian guides down the Hayes and Saskatchewan Rivers until he reached the area of present-day The Pas, Manitoba. There he wintered before striking out on foot across the plains and reaching Touchwood Hill near present-day Saskatoon, Saskatchewan. Some historians think he may have reached the Red Deer River in present-day southern Alberta.

Kelsey's journey lasted two years, and the young explorer hunted buffalo with the native peoples and lived off deer, fish, and birds, narrowly avoiding starvation several times. He spoke Cree and possibly Assiniboine and was renowned for his appreciation of native peoples. He is believed to be the first European to see the plains and meet with the plains natives.

Ultimately, Kelsey returned with many natives willing to trade at Hudson Bay. But his journey soon disappeared into near obscurity—the Hudson's Bay Company governor said Kelsey had not significantly affected company policy or business and refused to recognize publicly the trader's journey. Kelsey later became a senior supervisor and lived out his days in faithful service to the company.

the name the French used for their New World colony. La Vérendrye constructed fur-trading posts at Fort Maurepas (1734) on the southern shore of Lake Winnipeg, Fort Rouge (1737) near today's Winnipeg, Fort la Reine (1738) on the Assiniboine River near present-day Portage la Prairie, and Fort Dauphin (1741) at the southern end of Lake Winnipegosis. His sons made a notable journey down part of the Missouri River in the early 1740s into the present-day Dakotas and Montana. La Vérendrye's expansion of the French fur trade presented a serious challenge to the Hudson's Bay Company's monopoly and set the stage for long-term conflict in the area between French and British interests.

The Métis

The early forts and the trade between the aboriginal peoples and the fur traders gave rise to a new group of people, the Métis. Most of the first Métis resulted from the offspring of French fur traders and native women, although today the people are considered to include those who descend not only from French but also Scottish, English, Irish, and other unions with native peoples. The Métis were to figure prominently in the fur trade, in the battle between the rival companies, and ultimately in the formation of the province itself.

Written records are lacking on the beginnings of the Métis as an organized people in the area of present-day Manitoba, but researchers believe the Métis as a whole were noticed more and more as little as twenty years after the Europeans arrived. By the late 1700s and early 1800s, record keepers noted that they were an established presence.

Relations between Europeans and Métis peoples were difficult to manage from the beginning. The Métis were often skilled laborers raised around the fur trade forts, but they also retained much of their aboriginal heritage. Many hunted and lived nomadic lives, following the buffalo or other animals in season. Some of the early Métis were ultimately adopted back into native tribes, but those around the forts had a more difficult time. The Hudson's Bay Company, for instance, prevented employees whose contracts had expired from taking their children with them back to England. Abandoned children were then forced either to return to tribal living—difficult for many to do who had grown up in the forts—or rely on the mercy of the forts to provide for them. In this way, many Métis became valued employees of the forts and important traders, hunters, and trappers.

The Métis of French heritage likely appeared first around Lake Winnipeg and the early French forts. They, too, faced many of the difficulties of choosing between the nomadic life and the fort life. French influence in the areas outside of Quebec began to diminish after the British won the Seven Years' War in Europe, forcing the French, with the signing of the Treaty of Paris in 1763, to relinquish most of their New World colonies. In the 1780s the North West Company was formed. This new fur-trading rival of the Hudson's Bay Company was based in Montreal and was culturally more mixed (mostly Scottish and French-Canadian) than the

■ *Métis men dance in a camp near Pembina, Manitoba. Many Métis worked as traders for the North West Company.*

British-dominated Hudson's Bay Company. Métis tended to remain at the North West Company forts as traders, hunters, and trappers because they enjoyed greater personal freedom than they would have had in Hudson's Bay Company forts. Many Métis would also remain loyal to the North West Company when it eventually clashed violently with the Hudson's Bay Company.

The Birth of the North West Company

The French fur trade faltered badly during the Seven Years' War, leaving the Hudson's Bay Company with a short-lived monopoly. By the mid-1780s, Scottish and British investors formed the North West Company. It was determined to use an aggressive mix of French, native, and European traders to challenge the stodgy Hudson's Bay Company.

Taking over a number of forts from the French, the North West Company quickly established a strong presence in present-day southern Manitoba. The North West Company offered better incentives to its traders than did the Hudson's Bay Company, allowing the North Westers to grab larger pieces of the trade. The new competition forced the Hudson's Bay Company to reorganize and to more aggressively pursue expansion. It began to offer new incentives to its employees and give them greater freedom to make decisions. Further, the Hudson's Bay

Company began to consider promoting settlement as a means of expansion in the area around Lake Winnipeg.

The Companies' Bloody Competition

Before the early 1800s, forts and trading posts were the only settlements of the fur trade. The fur trade companies were not particularly interested in promoting farming communities, fearing that clearing of the land would reduce fur-bearing animals' habitat. But in 1811 the Hudson's Bay Company granted one of its part owners, the Scottish nobleman Thomas Douglas, fifth Earl of Selkirk, 116,000 square miles (300,000 square kilometers) of company land in the area surrounding present-day Winnipeg. Selkirk had gained a controlling interest in the Hudson's Bay Company to promote his emigration plans for landless Scottish peasants. By August 1812 an advance party from Scotland led by Miles Macdonell had arrived at the fork of the Red and Assiniboine Rivers to establish the Red River Colony (also known as Assiniboia). Over the next few years, settlers from England and Scotland poured in, and many Métis joined the settlement as well.

The Hudson's Bay Company no doubt recognized that this settlement would pose a major threat to North West dominance of the local fur trade. Settlers were positioned such that they could easily cut off trade routes of the North West Company. Further, new incentives offered by the Hudson's Bay Company initially drew many Métis laborers away from the North West forts to the settlement or to Hudson's Bay forts. Relationships that had been cordial at best between the two companies soured, and violence soon followed.

Attacks on the Red River Colony

The North West Company and the local Métis population soon found themselves in direct conflict with the Red River Colony over trade and settlement issues. During the first year of the colony's existence, a number of Métis families came to the settlement. Macdonell, appointed by Douglas governor of the colony, gave preferential treatment and the best land to settlers from Europe, however. This occurred at a time when

■ *Thomas Douglas, the fifth Earl of Selkirk, had a great influence in the settlement of the Red River Colony.*

the Métis were developing a stronger sense of self-identity as a people. Many Métis eventually came to view the colony as a threat to their sovereignty and to the way of life that they had enjoyed with the North West Company.

In the spring of 1815, the North West Company organized an attack on the settlement. "From 9 to 11 June 1815," writes Métis historian Marcel Giraud, "the palisades of the fort were subjected to a sustained and deadly fusillade which claimed several victims . . . the attackers could act with impunity, unconcerned about the fire of their adversaries, who were reduced to shooting at random against an invisible attacker in an atmosphere obscured by the smoke that on all sides floated out of the thickets where the assailants were hiding."[3]

Macdonell soon surrendered, and the homes and other buildings of the settlement were burned. Selkirk vowed, however, not to give up. By early 1816 he had appointed a new governor, Robert Semple, reestablished the Colony, and built a fort, dubbed Fort Douglas. This set the stage for a new and more violent round of confrontation, one that ultimately led to the rival companies' 1821 merger.

The Seven Oaks Incident

The Hudson's Bay Company renewed hostilities in the spring of 1816 when it seized Fort Gibraltar, a North West Company fort near the fork of the Red and Assiniboine Rivers. Semple declared that North Westers and their Métis allies would not be allowed passage on the Red River. On June 1 a group of Métis men and North West Company loyalists under the leadership of Métis captain Cuthbert Grant captured the Hudson's Bay Company post at Brandon House on the upper Assiniboine River. This event was a turning point, notes Friesen: "Before these struggles [the Métis] had simply been traders and hunters and employees, family members and relatives, but now they were a collective force, an association larger than a family and with more important bonds than a company; they were, as they described it, a new nation."[4]

The area was already a powder keg of tension between the rival trading companies, with the spark for the violence of the "Seven Oaks Incident" that occurred on June 19, 1816, ultimately being control of the season's pemmican.

In addition to plundering Brandon House, Grant and his men had seized a number of the Hudson's Bay Company's pemmican boats on the Qu'Appelle River. To prevent the Métis from transporting any pemmican over the Red and Assiniboine Rivers, Semple had set up soldiers along their banks. He also had a gunboat patrol the mouth of the Red at Lake Winnipeg. Grant and his men thus decided to transport their plundered pemmican overland, from the Assiniboine near present-day Portage la Prairie northeast to the Red, where they planned to meet up with some North Westers. The path of Grant's men took them close to Fort Douglas, where they were spotted by Salteaux Indians who alerted governor Semple. Semple led some twenty-five of his men out to confront Grant and the Métis. Semple apparently did not expect to fight, however, since he left his cannons behind.

On June 19, 1816, Grant sent Francois Boucher to meet Semple and demand his surrender. Boucher and Semple angered each other, and Semple grabbed the reins of Boucher's horse. Shots were fired, and the Métis quickly overwhelmed

■ Pemmican: The Food That Fed the Fur Trade

Pemmican, from a Cree word meaning "manufactured grease," is dried buffalo or other meat that has been pounded into a powder and then combined with melted fat. It is easily stored and transported in hide bags and thus became a staple food for fur traders.

The Métis had used their wily trading skills and their formidable buffalo-hunting knowledge to develop an extensive market for pemmican. They sold it to the U.S. Army as well as to fur traders and natives. Because the Selkirk colony settlers had been experiencing food shortages in recent winters, Macdonell in 1814 prohibited the export of pemmican from Assiniboia. This ban had a potentially devastating effect on many Métis peoples' livelihood. It also represented a direct challenge to North West Company traders, who had come to rely on Métis-supplied pemmican as a major part of their diet.

Semple's men, killing the governor and twenty others, while losing only one of their own. Many of Semple's men were mutilated after their deaths, and their bodies were left out on the plains, later to be buried by the Salteaux.

Historians have heatedly debated the events of the Seven Oaks Incident. Some say that it was a well-plotted attack carried out by Grant and the Métis, while others insist that it was clash brought on by happenstance and the mistaken wanderings of Grant and his men too close to Fort Douglas. Historians' cultural perspectives have also played a part. French and Métis histories refer to the incident as the Seven Oaks "battle," while it's still listed in the *Encyclopedia Britannica* as the Seven Oaks "massacre." One Métis writer says that Seven Oaks "is considered the historic moment when the Métis stood up as a nation and fought off oppression and encroachment of England through the Hudson's Bay Company."[5]

Over the short term, the incident caused increased bitterness on both sides. Within a year, forces under Lord Selkirk had attacked and captured the North West Company's Fort William. Selkirk also filed various lawsuits against the North West Company. The British sent a royal commissioner to investigate Grant's actions at Seven Oaks, but the charges were dismissed. It was only after Selkirk's death in 1820 that the Hudson's Bay and North West companies could successfully begin to negotiate a merger.

Resurgence of the Red River Colony

The 1821 merger changed forever this part of Rupert's Land, ending most of the violence if not the rivalry that had divided the area's people. The new era was also a harbinger of both the prosperity and the tensions that characterized Manitoba in the twentieth century. The Métis enjoyed new opportunities and at least temporarily controlled some land, but they competed with First Nations people and faced discrimination from others. First Nations peoples eventually saw their buffalo herds die and diseases ravage their tribes.

With competition pushed aside, the newly merged company (which retained the Hudson's Bay Company name) allowed the resettlement of the Red River area. It became a large and prosperous settlement for a diverse group of people, particularly the Métis. In 1821 the population was a mere four hundred, with about half from Scotland, one-third of

French descent, and the rest German or Swiss. The Germans and Swiss left within a few years and the European population in Red River grew slowly, numbering only one thousand in the mid-1840s. (By this time the Hudson's Bay Company had repurchased the territory from Selkirk's estate.) But the Métis came by the hundreds from the Pembina area, and by the early 1840s, they numbered about six thousand in the Red River and Assiniboine River areas.

The Métis settlements were marked by dual lifestyles. Many families established farms that they tended for parts of the year, only to leave for seasonal buffalo hunts. The Métis could be gone for months at a time, living as nomads, then return to their farms and resume their labors. Such patterns were a mystery to many Europeans in the colony and probably contributed to later tensions between the groups.

Racial Tensions Build

Tensions between Métis and European settlers were mirrored by those between the Métis and native peoples. After the 1821 merger, the Hudson's Bay Company increasingly turned to the Métis for supplies of buffalo meat and fur. The Métis became fierce competitors of the native peoples, eventually supplanting them as the primary processors of pemmican. The intense competition between the Métis and the First Nations peoples only heightened a growing problem—the thinning of the buffalo herds. The two groups found themselves chasing the herds farther and farther west, increasing the time and expense spent on the hunt.

Further, the public's perception of land and property shifted somewhat between the 1840s and the 1870s. First Nations peoples had viewed the land and its products not as private property but as communal resources. The growing numbers of Europeans who settled the area often drove native

■ *A Scottish Métis woman poses for the camera. The Red River Colony was resettled by a diverse group of people including Scots and Métis.*

peoples off lands, at times violently, and claimed the resources as their own. The Métis adopted many of these attitudes as well, conflicting with the Cree over buffalo hunting in the Qu'Appelle River area in eastern present-day Saskatchewan.

In addition to these tensions were those brought about by the vast social changes sweeping European thought, from social Darwinism ("only the fittest people survive") to religious supremacy ("only the Christian God is the true God"). European leaders in the Red River area laid out policies following the era's "Euro-centric" beliefs. For example, Friesen records that the Métis were never employed by the Hudson's Bay Company in leadership roles. He says, "Rather, the Métis were placed in the ranks of the labourers and were expected to man boats, build posts, hunt provisions, tend horses, chop wood, cut hay, and perform the countless other tasks associated with jacks-of-all-trades."[6] Christian missionaries in the Red River Colony praised farm life as morally superior to hunting and gathering. They also condemned as "unchristian" mixed-racial marriages. Such teachings contributed to social tensions and undermined ethnic pride.

The Emergence of the Métis Identity

The Métis in the Red River area ultimately broke free of the Hudson's Bay Company by challenging its monopoly. In 1849, an Assiniboia court tried Pierre Guillaume Sayer, a Métis of Red River, and three other Métis for illegally selling furs in competition with the Hudson's Bay Company. Sayer was found guilty by a jury of seven English speakers and five French speakers, but the huge Métis turnout at the trial caused the court to fear punishing him. Sayer and the others were released unsentenced amid cheers from the Métis throngs that "le commerce est libre."

With the Hudson's Bay Company's economic monopoly irreparably broken, the Métis suddenly were able to become more than menial laborers. They grew into entrepreneurs who traded their own furs, ran their own businesses, and served as guides and liaisons between other companies. With this pride developed a powerful Métis identity that saw the Métis as a separate nation, equal to the growing population of Europeans.

In 1867, an act of the British parliament created the new Dominion of Canada, with four provinces (Quebec, Ontario, Nova Scotia, and New Brunswick) opting for inclusion in a

■ Métis Rebel Leader Louis Riel

Louis Riel was born in the Red River settlement in 1844, the oldest of Louis and Julie Lagimodiere-Riel's eleven children. Riel's parents were deeply religious and politically prominent in the community (his father was among the leaders of the Métis who rallied to support Sayer), and Riel grew up speaking French and English. A bright student, Riel was sent to Montreal for religious instruction that he never completed. In 1864–1865 the death of his father and a failed romance caused deep despair.

Riel gave up his law education, wandered some in the United States, and returned to Red River in 1868. Riel's education and the Métis' fond memories of his father allowed Riel to quickly become a leader. In 1869, he led the taking of Fort Garry and established a provisional government. His execution of Thomas Scott, an accused assassin, enraged the federal government, and though Riel was elected to the House of Commons three times, he was unable to fill the seat. In 1875, he was exiled from Canada.

The years from 1875 to 1884 were marked by personal difficulty, including two stays in Quebec asylums. During those years, Riel became convinced that he had a religious duty to lead the Métis people. In 1884, a delegation of Métis leaders convinced Riel to take ongoing Métis concerns to the federal government, which were ignored. The short-lived 1885 rebellion resulted, and Riel was captured and tried for treason. He rejected his own attorneys' assertions that he was not guilty by reason of insanity, and a jury of six English Protestants found him guilty but recommended mercy. But Judge Hugh Richardson ordered his execution, and appeals were dismissed when the government deemed Riel sane. Riel was hanged on November 16, 1885, in Regina, and buried in St. Boniface.

■ *Louis Riel was exiled from Canada in 1875.*

new Canadian government. Canada quickly began to organize and assert control over its territory. British Protestant settlers poured into the Red River area, and the French-speaking Métis felt themselves threatened more and more, feeling that their status as business people and hunters would be taken away and that they would be stripped of their lands. Further, they wanted the rights to speak their own language, run their own schools, and maintain their culture.

All these tensions culminated in 1869, when the Canadian government negotiated to purchase Rupert's Land from the Hudson's Bay Company. The Métis rebelled when it appeared that this transfer of land, which included Métis-populated Assiniboia, would be accomplished with little or no input from them. Louis Riel, a young French-speaking Métis, led a group of Métis combatants who stormed (without resistance) the Hudson's Bay Company's Fort Garry and set up a provisional government. The Canadian government agreed to postpone the transfer of land from the Hudson's Bay Company and to negotiate with Métis representatives about the entry of Assiniboia into the confederation.

By May of 1870 the Métis had won concessions from the government that admitted Manitoba as a province—though much smaller in size than it is today—and secured the Métis certain rights. Ultimately, however, the benefits the Métis reaped from their rebellion were short-lived. After Riel approved the execution of an accused assassin, the Canadian government chased him into exile in the United States. The now-leaderless new province was faced with a struggle, which ultimately would prove futile, to remain a Métis society.

CHAPTER 3

Immigrants Shape the Province

T he Métis rebellion and subsequent formation of Manitoba did not solve the tensions between the Métis and incoming settlers, nor did it resolve crucial land claims. In reality, the Métis triumph was brief and the results mixed. Soon, government actions and the forces of immigration would marginalize the Métis. The 1870s and 1880s were marked by an influx of diverse settlers but also by an exodus of many of the Métis who had lived in the Red River valley. The completion of the transcontinental railroad encouraged further settlement, but economic recessions slowed progress. Still, the province recovered, grew, and eventually expanded, building the foundation of today's society.

The Decline of the Métis

The Métis rebellion failed to resolve many of the Métis-Canadian government disagreements, and the resulting struggles damaged Métis pride and strength in Manitoba for years to come. In the summer of 1870, immediately after agreeing to accept Manitoba as a province, the Canadian government sent an armed force under Garnet Wolseley as a "mission of peace." The Métis saw it instead as a show of force. Friesen cites this period as a particularly dark chapter in Métis history: "The fate of the Métis in Manitoba, particularly those who were French-speaking, was sad. From the moment

Wolseley's troops streamed into Upper Fort Garry, the Métis were made to feel strangers in their own land. Catcalls and fistfights in front of Winnipeg's saloons were simply the most visible signs of a process that ended in exile for some, silence and shame for others."[7]

While the Métis had demanded land guarantees from the government, the federation granted only 1.4 million acres of land to Métis children, not established Métis families. Unlike its policy with the original four provinces, the federal government also retained control over Manitoba's public lands and natural resources. (The federal government also took this approach to Alberta and Saskatchewan when they were established in 1905; it was not until 1930 that all three provinces were granted control over their lands and resources.) Further, deciding where the Métis land would be was difficult. The government wanted to use the best lands to attract the settlers that were beginning to stream into the country from Europe. Many of the Métis were nomadic, following the buffalo herds farther and farther west as they disappeared from the central plains. The government thus deemed these Métis ineligible to keep their land titles. It seized the land, displacing thousands and forcing them to move west.

In other instances, the government offered land scrips, or payments that could be used to buy dominion land, to the Métis. But the scrips program, in most instances, was a disaster. Land prospectors bought up many scrips. The Métis saw few of the lands to which they were entitled, and the money they received amounted to very little.

Thousands of Métis migrated west and settled in areas around Edmonton and southern present-day Alberta. Many followed the disappearing buffalo herds, while others sought only lands on which to begin farming anew. The composition and power structure in Manitoba was permanently changed. At its formation in 1870, the province had approximately twelve thousand residents. About half were French-speaking Métis, one-third were English-speaking Métis, and less than one-sixth were European or Canadian in origin. The flight of the Métis and the influx of new settlers caused a dramatic reversal. By 1886, only 7 percent of the 109,000 people in the province were Métis, whether English- or French-speaking, and nearly 70 percent of the people were of Irish, Scottish, or British descent.

A Shifting Political Balance

Few events changed Manitoba more than the arrival of the railroad. In 1881, business and city leaders in Winnipeg out-maneuvered rival cities and convinced the Canadian Pacific Railway to run its transcontinental line through their city. The Winnipeg station began the transformation of Winnipeg from a trading outpost to a vital farm- and ranch-product shipping center and eventually to a bustling, cosmopolitan city. In 1870, the city had as few as two hundred residents; by 1886, the city had twenty thousand residents.

The regional balance shifted, as well, during this time. In 1871, the Red and Assiniboine River areas contained more than two-thirds of the provincial population. By 1886, that percentage had dropped to 40 percent, with many of the new-comers bringing distinctive cultures to the area. For instance, two Mennonite settlements grew up around Portage la Prairie and Gladstone. (In 1881 provincial and federal authorities had agreed upon an extension of Manitoba's borders, mainly westward and northward, that increased the province's size five-fold. Manitoba's current borders and size, however, weren't to be finalized until 1912.)

The bulk of the incoming settlers during this period were Irish, Scottish, and British, and tensions flared between them and the French-speaking people already established in the

■ *Winnipeg in 1871 shows signs of its transition from out-post to bustling city.*

■ The Manitoba School Question of 1890

The federal Manitoba Act of 1870, which had brought the province into existence, had protected French as an official language and guaranteed separate schools for the (predominantly Catholic) French. Two decades later, however, (predominantly Protestant) British- and English-speaking residents were firmly in the majority in Manitoba. Some Manitoba politicians believed that the French were paying fewer tax dollars than the British and that French schools were receiving larger grants from the treasury. Other Manitoba politicians opposed French loyalty to an increasingly powerful Catholic clergy. Great Britain remained a military and industrial world power, and British Canadians in Manitoba and other provinces were proclaiming British culture as the force that would lead the country in a new era of progress and growth.

The government of Manitoba was thus emboldened to establish English as the province's principal language. It also sought to replace the existing system of French-Catholic and British-Protestant schools with non-denominational schools. The movement met forceful resistance from the French-speaking population, which feared that the actions would make it very difficult to pass along the French heritage to young people.

Brit-power prevailed. In 1890 the provincial government overrode French objections and passed two bills that established a secular school system like that in the United States and made English the only official language (a status English enjoyed until 1984, when the provincial government returned French to equal status with English). The bills also reinforced inherent tensions within the province and paved the way for decades of lawsuits and political dissent.

province. The new settlers were fleeing the hardships in Europe—smaller land portions, illness, and oppression. They found solidarity and wide-open lands in Manitoba but also resentment from the established French cultures. The uneasy relations between French- and English-speakers culminated in the late 1880s in a famous clash over language and schools.

During the 1880s it became clear that the federal government, perhaps in part because it regretted the compromises that had been forced upon it when Manitoba was established, was continually looking for ways to extend its power and hold over the province. Ottawa's steps to encourage widespread immigration, however, were affected by the province's volatile economy.

A Boom-and-Bust Economy

While tensions between English and French mounted, the new agricultural economy suffered severe fluctuations. The arrival of the Canadian Pacific Railway in Winnipeg caused the city's real estate values to soar. Speculators and real estate agents made huge sums of money off incoming settlers who poured into the area and bought new farms. The exploding values could not last. Severe flooding of the Red River valley in April of 1882 destroyed crops and decimated land values. The resulting recession dragged on for several years, forcing hundreds of businesses to fold and slowing immigration through the 1880s.

But Winnipeg and Manitoba responded. Farmers continued to produce grain, and amongst at least some of them, they saw the provincial land as full of promise. In a letter to his mother, Edward Folkes, an immigrant from Norfolk, England, wrote of his land just north of Winnipeg: "Plough the land up, and you have a garden richly manured, to grow whatever you want. Every kind of fruit, almost, grows wild. Beautiful hay for the trouble of cutting and carving. . . . Days too short in winter, too long in summer—winter too long, summer too short. This is the only one objection the most prejudiced person can bring against this magnificent country."[8] On the strengths of such farmers and immigrants, the provincial economy gradually recovered. Manitoba braced itself for the next wave of immigrants and a new era of diversity.

The Expanding Province

In 1896, the federal government launched its boldest initiative to fill the prairies with productive settlers who would send grain to the east and in turn buy eastern manufactured goods. Minister of the Interior Clifford Sifton launched a publicity campaign in Europe to attract Scots, Scandinavians, Germans, and British. In response to one Dublin writer who characterized Manitoba as similar to Siberia, Sifton published pamphlets that hailed Manitoba in exaggerated terms. Historian Pierre Berton writes that "snow was never mentioned in the blizzard of pamphlets his department issued. 'Cold' was another taboo word. The accepted adjectives were 'bracing' and 'invigorating.' Why, it was so mild, one pamphlet declared, that 'the soft maple' could grow five feet in a single season! And if prospective immigrants confused the Manitoba maple, a weed tree, with the Eastern hardwood—Canada's symbol—too bad."[9]

Pamphlets like Sifton's had powerful effects on the poverty-stricken but strong-willed people they were aimed at. In much of the Austro-Hungarian empire in Europe, people such as the Poles and Ukrainians suffered from low wages, scarce land, and high taxes. Hearing of cheap land in Canada, more than one hundred and eighty thousand Ukrainians emigrated to Canada, settling mostly in the northern woodlands that stretched from Manitoba to Alberta. Thousands of these immigrants preferred the Manitoba forests to the plains—

■ The Ukrainians in Manitoba

The first two Ukrainians of the great Ukrainian immigration to Manitoba that took place from 1896 to 1914 were Vasyl Eleniak and Ivan Pylypiw. They arrived in Montreal in 1891 and traveled west to view the farmlands of the prairies. They returned to the Ukraine and gave friends and neighbors glowing reports. When Eleniak and Pylypiw returned to Canada, they brought many fellow Ukrainians with them. Later, the Ukrainian agriculture professor Joseph Oleskiw visited Canada and wrote an encouraging booklet, *About Free Lands,* that helped trigger a flood of immigration. Most of the Ukrainian immigrants to Canada settled in Manitoba and the other prairie provinces.

Whole blocs of the early Ukrainians came from various provinces of the Austro-Hungarian empire, particularly Galicia and Bukovina. A common heritage, however, and the need to put down roots united them. They built Manitoba's first Ukrainian church, St. Michael's Orthodox Church, in Gardenton in 1899. Today many onion-domed Ukrainian Catholic and Greek Orthodox churches can be spied throughout Manitoba.

The early immigrants suffered terribly. They received little government assistance beyond the promised quarter-section (160 acres) of land. In most cases, they were essentially put out on the prairies to fend for themselves. The infant mortality rate was extraordinarily high. To survive, many tried farming while others joined logging, mining, and railroad camps. In time, the Ukrainians built up a network of settlements with names like Zhoda ("harmony") and Komarno ("mosquito") that helped ease the transition for later immigrants.

■ *A Ukrainian church in southeast Manitoba reflects the diversity of cultures that settled in the area.*

wood was a rare and important commodity in their homeland. Though their first years were difficult, these immigrants were to play a crucial role in Manitoba's logging and mining operations over the next century.

Similarly, other immigrants poured in from eastern Europe. In 1898, the Doukhobors, a religious sect devoted to universal brotherhood and somewhat similar to the Mennonites and Quakers in their communal practices, faced strong persecution in their native Russia. Hearing of free land in Canada, more than seventy-five hundred emigrated in a five-month span. They lived temporarily in shelters in Winnipeg and eventually moved on to settlements in Saskatchewan and the western edge of Manitoba.

Across the province, others poured in as well. Jewish immigrants made a home for themselves in Winnipeg's North End, which also came to harbor most of the city's Slavs and Scandinavians. Later, the Hutterites, another religious sect, like the Doukhobors and the Mennonites settled in large numbers in southern Manitoba. The English, Irish, and Scottish continued to flow in and fill much of the Red River valley and other southern farm areas. American farmers moved north seeking cheaper land and better farming opportunities. The Chinese came in the 1880s to help build the Canadian Pacific Railway, but many chose to stay after its completion. Nearly thirty thousand lived on the prairies in 1900, with Manitoba home to several thousand of those.

Life for the New Immigrants

Life for these immigrant groups was difficult. As their numbers increased, an anti-immigrant backlash developed among the British population. The Ukrainians were accused of having low morals and engaging in wild criminality. In reality, Ukrainian crime was virtually nonexistent in Manitoba. In 1899, of the 1,205 criminals held in Winnipeg prisons, 1,037 were Canadians, 168 were foreign born, and only 9 were Ukrainian. The *Winnipeg Telegram* wrote that Slavic immigrants came from a "primitive" culture "whose customs are repulsive."[10] As writer Bruce Cherney has noted, "Some Winnipeggers went as far as to demand the government institute a system to exclude Slavs or, at least, a limitation on the number

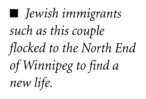

■ *Jewish immigrants such as this couple flocked to the North End of Winnipeg to find a new life.*

apr 20/1910

alberton

KEEP THE NEGRO ACROSS THE LINE

THE WINNIPEG BOARD OF TRADE TAKES DECIDED ACTION

Not Good Settlers or Agreeable Neighbors Either

Winnipeg, Man., April 19.—The Winnipeg board of trade this evening passed a strongly worded resolution, which will be forwarded to Ottawa, condemning the admission of negroes into Canada as settlers.

It is set forth in the resolution that these new-comers are not successful farmers nor agreeable neighbors for white settlers. The board also passed a resolution similar to that of the Manufacturers' association on the proposal to amend the railway act to enable the railway commission to suspend railway tariffs or charges on appeals from patrons of the railways against which grievances are held.

■ *A 1910 newspaper article condemns Negro settlement in Canada.*

allowed to immigrate to Canada. Sifton's prized immigrants were having a difficult time gaining acceptance in Canada."[11]

Other immigrant groups were facing similar challenges. Immigrants from Iceland arrived in Manitoba in 1875 and built a self-governing community on the western shore of Lake Winnipeg. The Republic of New Iceland, as the residents called it, formed a school, an Icelandic newspaper, and churches. They survived harsh conditions—even a smallpox epidemic—with little outside help. Ultimately, their settlement, like the Ukrainians', was integrated as other peoples arrived. (Plenty of Manitoba towns still have notable concentrations, however, of people with Ukrainian, Icelandic, and other ethnic backgrounds.)

The Chinese also faced problems and restrictions. Nearly all who emigrated were male, and they were generally confined to railway, restaurant, or laundry jobs. Further, laws directed at Chinese immigrants discouraged their integration into the larger population. For example, a Manitoba law passed in the first years of the twentieth century prevented white women from working in Chinese restaurants.

The Jews in Winnipeg's North End suffered poverty and persecution. Many who started out as unskilled laborers, garment workers, peddlers, and rag collectors nevertheless soon became tailors and small business owners.

Two Economic Expansions

Despite its growing pains, Manitoba began to develop strong rural communities and to adjust to its increasing diversity. From 1900 to 1914, Winnipeg was the gateway to the west, and Manitoba as a whole benefited. The Canadian Pacific, Canadian Northern, and the Grand Trunk Pacific railways all passed through Winnipeg. By 1911, some two dozen rail lines fanned out from Winnipeg, and it became a regional center for agricultural shipping, manufacturing, food processing, and other industries. The city grew its own financial district, complete with banks and insurance companies, ensuring its status as a national power.

In the meantime mining and logging operations began to flourish in the forests. The dramatic expansion of Manitoba lands northward by more than five hundred miles (eight hundred kilometers) in 1912 increased its population by approximately six thousand and hardened the provincial government's resolve to acquire control over the abundant natural resources from the federal government. In the south, farmers and ranchers flourished, using the cheap shipping available in Winnipeg to ship food all over the world.

■ *The expansion of Manitoba's economy led to a thriving lumber business. Here lumberjacks stack tree trunks headed for the lumberyard.*

■ The Canal That Cooled Manitoba

The completion of the Panama Canal in 1914 dealt a harsh blow to Winnipeg and to the economy of Manitoba as a whole. Before the canal, Winnipeg had been a crucial rail junction for grain and other goods shipped from farmers in the west to the eastern cities of both Canada and the United States. When the Panama Canal was completed, the Canadian government quickly built a large grain elevator at Vancouver's port. Suddenly it became cheaper for farmers in much of the west to ship goods to Vancouver for loading onto boats that could use the Panama Canal to reach the eastern seaboard of North America as well as Europe. Within two years, the first shipments of wheat from Canada to the United Kingdom arrived on the American freighter *War Viceroy*. By the mid-1920s, Vancouver was handling Alberta's entire agricultural output and much of Saskatchewan's, and Vancouver wholesaler agents were canvassing the west seeking more business.

In 1914, the beginning of World War I sent tremors through the Canadian economy. Some provinces prospered, and others were hurt. Manitoba, at least initially, did well. Wheat and grain were crucial military staples, and the prices of farm products soared, boosting the agricultural sector. Banking and financing companies also thrived, as farmers took out loans for new materials and new equipment to meet demand.

With the end of the war came falling grain prices and economic problems. Already in 1914, the shipping industry was in trouble because of the completion of the Panama Canal. Western shippers moved materials through Vancouver where boats took goods south to the canal and onto the rest of the world. New cities with railroad connections, like Edmonton, Alberta, competed fiercely for industry work and eroded Winnipeg's previously held shipping monopoly. Plummeting grain prices in 1920 triggered unrest among farmers. Perhaps more troubling, though, were the disparities in lifestyles that ultimately gave way to a period of tumult and upheaval in Manitoba's social systems.

The Canal was not the only development that set Winnipeg back. Calgary won a key Canadian Pacific Railway shop in 1912, and Regina landed a General Motors plant in 1928. Further, competing cities managed to strip Winnipeg of its freight discounts that had made shipping through Winnipeg so affordable. With these developments, Winnipeg ultimately became more a provincial and regional power than a national power.

Living Disparities and Social Upheaval

While the strong agricultural and shipping economy of the early twentieth century benefited many in Manitoba, thousands of others were essentially left behind, opening the door to huge unrest. Standards of living differed wildly across the province. Wealthy corporate managers and owners lived ostentatiously. Friesen notes that in 1912, twenty-six homes with a value of $20,000 or more—a huge sum for the times—were built in

■ The General Strike of 1919

The small victory labor had won with a threatened strike in 1918 had emboldened unionized employees in Winnipeg, but it had made business owners far more rigid. Company managers were looking for a chance to break the powerful unions, and that chance came with the 1919 strike.

When thirty thousand workers walked off the job on May 15, demanding better wages and working conditions, the city virtually came to a halt. Bread and milk deliveries, train service, police and fire coverage, and other essentials halted. Quickly, a strikers' council authorized the limited restoration of some services. The ironically named Unionist federal government led by Prime Minister Robert Borden, however, became alarmed that the workers had such power over the city. The government's subsequent involvement in the negotiations and the political wrangling that followed was to prove disastrous for the striking workers.

Representatives of the federal government went to Winnipeg and met with the city's manufacturers, bankers, and politicians, though not with the striking workers. The federal government then demanded that federal employees, such as postal workers and telephone workers, immediately return to work or be fired. Finally, on June 17 the government arrested ten strike leaders, essentially gutting the unions' leadership.

Although these actions had not halted the strike, the two sides seemed to be nearing a compromise that would call for only minor concessions from employers. But when the compromise was about to be reached, the city government authorized a return of streetcar service, triggering a mass demonstration on Portage Avenue and Main Street on June 21. The mayor came out to the City Hall steps after seeing the crowds' refusal to disperse. He read the Riot Act from the steps and unleashed the Northwest Mounted Police. They charged into a crowd of strikers, injuring thirty people and killing one (four police were also injured). Within a week of "Bloody Saturday," the strike collapsed.

Winnipeg. The wealthy enjoyed exclusive social clubs and controlled provincial and city politics. They tended to be of British origin, and they tried to impose their language, schooling systems, and religious beliefs on the incoming immigrants and on native peoples.

■ Dissatisfied workers march on the streets of Winnipeg during the 1919 workers' strike.

The wealthy corporate owners of the time also tended to deny their workers livable wages, proper working conditions, and social benefits. In consequence, working class people often lived from day to day. A 1909 government survey in Winnipeg found 837 people (120 families) living in forty-one houses—essentially, on average, three families and nine or ten boarders squeezed into one seven-room house. Often these houses were on narrow, twenty-five-foot-wide lots set up to maximize developers' profits. Winnipeg's substandard public water system was responsible for high rates of diseases such as typhoid. Winnipeg's poor North End in 1913 had higher infant death rates—almost one death for every four births—than most other major cities in the world. In the north, laborers worked through grueling weather and lived in remote camps far from their families. In southern rural areas, farmers saddled with high debts faced foreclosure.

Disenchanted workers in the cities soon formed strong unions. In general, northern laborers were too loosely organized to unionize, but farmers united in the south. The farmers and city workers created a powerful voting bloc. In 1918, union leaders threatened a general strike among Winnipeg city workers and won concessions from employers. Emboldened by this small victory, the unions staged a massive strike in 1919. They effectively halted government and business activity and provoked a major confrontation with city officials.

Farmers were more successful at implementing social and political change. Riled by what they saw as industry domination of the province, farmers helped form the progressive movement under the leadership of agricultural academic John Bracken. The coalition of progressive farmers and unionists elected Bracken first to the provincial legislature and then, in 1922, as premier, where he served for the next twenty-one years. Bracken's progressive provincial government sought to restore low freight rates for grain shipping, even while rates and tariffs for other industries remained higher. It also supported moderate hydroelectric development, logging, and mining in the north.

To the Present Day

The Panama Canal and the loss of the shipping monopoly eroded Winnipeg's power such that it inevitably became a provincial and regional power with less influence on the nation. Immigration tapered off over the decades, nearly ending in the Great Depression, and population growth picked up only somewhat in the decades to follow. In 1941, Manitoba's population was seven hundred and thirty thousand. By 1961, it was nine hundred and twenty thousand, and it now stands at a little more than one million one hundred thousand.

Most of Manitoba's growth has been concentrated in the Winnipeg metropolitan area. From 1940 to today, Winnipeg has more than doubled, thanks in large part to a shift from a rural economy to a more industrialized, city-based economy. Still, the growth of Winnipeg did not diminish economic development elsewhere. Mining, logging, and power generation have increased over the decades in the north, and towns like The Pas and Thompson have grown stronger over the years with this increased activity. This economic strength and diversity is reflected in the everyday lives of the province's people.

Life in Manitoba Today

Modern Manitoba retains much of the rural character and social diversity that marked its beginnings. Farmers still harvest crops from the rich, dark soils while immigrants from various nations work in Winnipeg's manufacturing, construction, and transportation industries. In addition, Manitoba has seen rapid expansion over the last decade in its high-tech, communications, and finance sectors. The daily lives of Manitoba's residents thus range from contemporary city life in Winnipeg, complete with sophisticated cultural attractions as well as attractive urban parks, to rural life in the remote north.

A Diverse and Educated Work Force

As has been true since the coming of the transcontinental railway, Winnipeg is not only the province's governmental capital but also its economic and cultural capital. The people are diverse not only in ethnic backgrounds but also in their occupations and family lives. Agriculture, manufacturing, and high-tech industries all support each other in Winnipeg and provide a strong base for the rest of the province.

Accounting for almost 60 percent of the provincial population, the Winnipeg metropolitan area includes people from widely different backgrounds. Just over 40 percent are of English or Canadian origin, but Germans, Scots, Ukrainians, French, and Irish each contribute roughly 10 percent of the city's population. Winnipeg residents overwhelmingly speak English, with about 75 percent claiming it as their first language. But nearly 25 percent of Winnipeg's people claim some

■ *Cattle ranching is
a staple of Manitoba's
economy.*

other language as their first language: French, German,
Ukrainian, Cree, Tagalog (Filipino), Polish, or others.

The diversity in people is mirrored by the many different
occupations that Winnipeg residents hold. Because Winnipeg is the provincial capital, it abounds in opportunities for
government workers, social workers, and educators. About
eighty-five thousand of the more than three hundred thousand employable people work in one of those three areas.
Manufacturing and retailing provide another eighty thousand
jobs, while business and financial institutions account for approximately seventy thousand jobs. Agricultural and food industries are important for the province. The city is home to
the head office of the Canadian Wheat Board and to numerous
grain and livestock companies. Manufacturers build equipment for farming, food processing, and heavy industry, and
growth in secondary manufacturing has been ten times the national average since 1991. The city is also home to numerous
insurance and banking institutions, making it a regional financial center.

Higher education is important among Winnipeg workers.
More than 44 percent of Manitobans over the age of fifteen

have obtained some post-secondary education in universities, community colleges, or trade schools, and the figure is even higher within the Winnipeg metro area. High education levels translate to better income—average annual income in Winnipeg is more than $50,000. More than 60 percent of Winnipeg residents own their dwellings. Almost three in every five dwellings are houses, with residents typically having two or more bedrooms per residence.

Preserving Winnipeg's Heritage

Winnipeg's relative prosperity allows its residents time to enjoy their surroundings—both those they have built and those that are natural. The city has worked hard to preserve its natural heritage. It is home to 850 parks, and many of the larger parks have been preserved as recreational space. Mature trees and bushes are common in parks and in neighborhoods, giving the city plenty of greenery.

Winnipeg offers a wide range of attractions and activities. Kildonan Park on the banks of the Red River has Canada's longest-running outdoor theater, Rainbow Stage, as well as a swimming pool, public boating dock, and other facilities. Park visitors can walk among some of the oldest and largest trees in Manitoba or take the children to visit "Hansel and Gretel's Witch Hut."

Downtown, Winnipeg Square is the center of the shopping district and offers numerous stores and services. The nearby Exchange District, named after the Winnipeg Grain and Produce Exchange founded in 1887, was the city's warehouse and wholesale business district when it was built during the prosperous era at the beginning of the twentieth century. The district also housed the booming city's "newspaper row" as well as opulent hotels and theaters. Today the thirty-block Exchange District presents an eclectic assortment of antique shops, bookstores, sidewalk cafes, art galleries, and boutiques. At night, the many bars, nightclubs, and restaurants of Old Market Square in the Exchange District make it a vibrant hub of activity. Many of the cut-stone and terra-cotta commercial buildings have been lovingly preserved, and the city boasts that the district has "the most extensive collection of turn-of-the-century architecture on the continent."[12]

St. Boniface, Winnipeg's charming French district, perhaps best exemplifies the city's surprising cultural diversity. Annexed by Winnipeg in 1972, St. Boniface during its early history housed much of the area's French and Métis population, and it is still a stronghold of French speakers. It is home to gothic-arched St. Boniface Cathedral and to St. Boniface Museum, which holds numerous fur trade relics.

Winnipeg is ultimately the heart and soul of the province, encapsulating the province's various languages, lifestyles, and occupations. Its residents enjoy a mixture of big-city living and natural beauty. They have a good standard of living and tend to have good wages. Their relations with each other can be somewhat tense, but on the whole they represent fairly the western province.

Manitoba's "Second City"

Manitoba's second-largest city, Brandon, is not on a par with Winnipeg, having a population of only forty thousand people and far fewer cultural opportunities. But Brandon, located in the heart of western Manitoba's farm country (two-thirds of the province's farmland is within 80 miles/130 kilometers) and due south of Riding Mountain National Park, is nevertheless a lively agricultural hub with interesting attractions. Situated on the Assiniboine River, the Trans-Canada Highway, and the Canadian Pacific Railway, Brandon is a major trade and transportation center for wheat, cattle, and other products. The city itself is a blend of small-town department stores, eateries, and service businesses, and urban elements such as Brandon College and the Commonwealth Air Training Plan Museum at the municipal airport, complete with various historic but working aircraft.

Brandon's main industries are driven by agriculture. Manufacturers make and sell fertilizer, farm equipment, and other agriculture-related products. Residents can enjoy a range of activities at the Keystone Center, a huge recreational complex with five arenas, livestock spaces, convention spaces, and a curling club. Residents can also golf at one of several courses or play sports such as baseball, soccer, and football at the area's numerous fields and parks. Brandon is the site of one of the province's first experimental farms, started in 1886 and continuing now as the federal Agriculture and Agri-Food Canada Research Station.

A Grain-Growing Center

In stark contrast to Manitoba's few cities are the many tiny rural towns that dot the provincial landscape. In the southern parts of the province, many of these towns are devoted to producing huge volumes of grain. Life in these traditional agricultural communities is dictated to a great degree by the seasons and one's role in the community.

■ Western Canada's Largest French-Speaking Community

In all of western Canada, Manitoba has the highest percentage of people who speak French, and much of the province's infrastructure caters to French speakers' needs. For example, Manitoba has one of the strongest networks of Francophone (French-speaking) financial institutions, the caisses populaires, outside of Quebec, and in 1994 the province established a new Francophone School Division. The heart of Manitoba's French-speaking community is St. Boniface, the French quarter in Winnipeg.

Although a municipal ward of the city of Winnipeg, St. Boniface remains a distinct community, both tight-knit and anxious to show its culture and heritage to the rest of the province and nation. It is home to the only university in the west providing instruction entirely in French, Le Collège Universitaire de St. Boniface. (Three other Manitoba colleges offer instruction in both French and English.) The St. Boniface Cathedral is the most recent of four churches dating back to 1818, when St. Boniface was founded as a Roman Catholic mission. The cathedral is now one of the most imposing church structures in western Canada. Much of the powerful 1906 cathedral that was gutted in a 1968 fire remains—the sacristy, facade, and walls were all incorporated into the 1972 design. The cemetery in the front of the cathedral includes the grave of Louis Riel.

St. Boniface General Hospital, established in 1871 by the Sisters of Charity of Montreal "Grey Nuns," is a university-affiliated hospital serving not only Manitobans but also people from Saskatchewan and northern Ontario as well. It remains devoted to the charitable purposes for which it was founded. St. Boniface is also the site of Francophone media outlets, performing arts groups, and community organizations.

■ Riding Mountain National Park

Manitoba's most popular national park, Riding Mountain is located west of Lake Manitoba and south of Dauphin Lake, about a three-hour drive from Winnipeg or one hour from Brandon. An important preserve of prairie and woodland, Riding Mountain National Park includes a dramatic section of the Manitoba Escarpment, the prominent land formation that rises from the prairie as travelers head northwest across the province. The park provides habitat for bear, plains buffalo, moose, and beaver. Balsam firs and mountain maples grow prominently.

The land was originally home to the Ojibway tribe, which hunted, trapped, and traded furs in the region. When the reserve system was started in the 1870s, several First Nations groups settled around the park. A 1991 land claim by the Ojibway restored to them a disputed fishing reserve, and some of the park land is still disputed as part of a native land claim.

The park is a major recreational attraction for the central rural area. Boating is permitted on Clear Lake, Lake Audy, and Moon Lake, while other smaller lakes are open to nonmotorized craft. The sparkling waters and sandy beaches of Clear Lake are the park's most popular swimming sites. Backpacking is permitted throughout the park, and hikers savor the views of expansive evergreens in the central section of the park, and the dramatic gorges in the east. Cycling, canoeing, horseback riding, and cross-country skiing are also popular tourist and recreational activities in the park.

Each town or municipality has its own character, but Manitou, home to about eight hundred people just north of the border from the states of Minnesota and North Dakota, is typical. The town's economy is based almost entirely on agriculture, with farmers producing wheat and other grains, repair people servicing farm equipment, and retail outlets catering to farm-related as well as everyday needs. Outside of farming, the area supports a modest tourism sector, attracting people to the wildlife in the area and to a small ski resort (the slopes are thanks to the escarpment) that also offers a nine-hole golf course during the summer. Within the town, there are just over three hundred mostly modest houses, about two-thirds of which were built before 1960, and no apartments. In general, Manitou families are conventional two-parent families with several children.

Life in the rural farm towns of southern Manitoba is rooted in the crops, seasonal rhythms, and in some cases even the dwellings that date back to the province's origins. Wheat is still king, accounting for more than 40 percent of production value among all Manitoba crops, but other crops are grown as well. Canola in particular is beginning to rival wheat in importance. (Canola, derived from "Canada" and "oil" and also known as rapeseed, is a seed crop used to make a versatile food oil.) For example, the rural town of Carman, south of Portage la Prairie and site of the Canadian Canola Growers Association, specializes in seed farming, including canola and sunflower.

Life in the Northern Forests

The northern towns that have benefited from the expansion of mining and forestry differ markedly from southern farming towns in setting. Towns from the two areas, however, often share a reliance on one major industry and a populace willing to face hardships. The wilderness that surrounds northern towns does provide more opportunities to attract visitors from the province and beyond. Like the farmers in the south, the residents of Manitoba's north are a tough breed, often engaging in challenging work in harsh conditions.

The city of Thompson, located in the center of the province and often called the gateway to the north, is a prototype for the northern "company town." Thompson did not exist at all in 1956 when employees of Inco, a leading Canadian mineral company, discovered a rich deposit of nickel ore near Moak Lake in central Manitoba. Provincial officials agreed to build a town and a railway link to Churchill on the Hudson Bay. Thompson, named after Inco's chairman, sprang into being in the late 1950s, backed by Inco's construction and operation of what was the first integrated mining, smelting, and refining nickel complex.

Thompson quickly grew to a population of more than twenty thousand during the 1960s, though increased competition in the nickel market in recent years has caused its economy to slow somewhat and the population to shrink to about thirteen thousand. The town has enjoyed only limited success at attracting additional, non-mining business. Long-term planning by provincial officials has ensured that Thompson's citizens enjoy all the services of other towns, from public education to modern health care facilities. Many of Thompson's residents work for Inco or for businesses and services related to the nickel mining. Other workers provide retail and business services.

■ Mennonite Millionaires

Named for the Dutch priest Menno Simons, the Mennonite religion grew out of a sixteenth-century Protestant reform movement in Europe. Mennonites fleeing persecution in Eastern Europe came to America in 1683, and in 1786, a gradual emigration from Pennsylvania to Canada started. In the 1870s, seven thousand Dutch Mennonites who had settled for a time in Russia came to Manitoba. Later, in the 1920s, after the Russian Revolution, another twenty thousand came from Russia and settled across the prairies.

Today, traditional Mennonites in parts of Canada and the United States avoid motorized vehicles and shun contemporary entertainment, preferring a simple agricultural lifestyle. But in southern Manitoba, a short distance from Winnipeg, Mennonites' traditional work ethic has been combined with a more liberal lifestyle to create a number of multimillion-dollar industries. Many Mennonites in southern Manitoba embrace modern technology and appliances, and the result has been fruitful. In tiny Altona, an hour south of Winnipeg, book printer Friesens Corporation printed 25 million books in two plants (including nine hundred thousand copies of the latest Harry Potter book) and employs six hundred people. Company leaders estimate that sales have approached $100 million.

Similarly, in Winkler, a short drive west of Altona, the private Mennonite company Triple E Industries makes recreational vehicles (RVs) and highway trailers. Last year, the company shipped about one thousand RVs and about fifteen hundred trailers. Across the Red River to the east, in Steinbach, Mennonite-owned Loewen Enterprises ships about six hundred premium windows per day, furnishing some of the finest homes on the continent.

Such business successes have been attributed to the Mennonites' close-knit society and to their strong work ethic. For example, Mennonites tend to have few absences at work and to maintain high productivity. The so-called millionaire Mennonites also seem to be socially conscious, with a number of them reinvesting their wealth in their communities. Friesens, for example, is paying for a hockey arena and water park in Altona, and Triple E is expanding a church in Winkler. Friesens also generously sets aside 10 percent of its pretax profits for its employees.

Thompson is surrounded by striking Canadian Shield wilderness that provides ample opportunities for hiking, canoeing, fishing, and camping. In the winter, residents enjoy snowmobiling, cross-country skiing, and ice fishing. Nearby Paint Lake Provincial Park is a scenic recreational site that attracts beachgoers, fishing enthusiasts, and motorboaters. In Thompson's modern recreation center, residents can relax or try their hand at curling, racquetball, hockey, and other sports.

The Pas is a small Manitoba town (population six thousand) whose demographics are somewhat similar to Thompson's but whose history is very different. The Pas is located on the south bank of the Saskatchewan River (the town's name is thought to derive from a Cree word for "a narrowing in the river") near Manitoba's border with Saskatchewan. Some of Manitoba's earliest European explorers, including Henry Kelsey, visited the site of The Pas. By the mid-1700s The Pas had become a fur trade center and the site of a French fort. In the twentieth century it became a major logging town.

The Pas is located strategically on the edge of the Canadian Shield and on the railway between Churchill and points south. This has allowed it to develop into a trade and transportation site for the farming to the south and the west, mining and fishing to the north, and tourism from all directions. Town residents market crops, build and repair farm equipment, and sell products to the farming industries. The thick

■ *A truck stops on Churchill's main road during a cold winter. Residents in this part of Canada must endure a harsh climate.*

forests provide jobs to many who work in logging and timber processing. The forests also attract wilderness enthusiasts who come to hike and camp. Like Thompson, The Pas also offers a host of in-town recreational opportunities.

Manitoba's northernmost town is Churchill. Situated on the Hudson Bay and home to about one thousand residents, it is some seven hundred miles (eleven hundred kilometers) due north of Manitoba's southern prairie towns. Churchill is closer, in fact, to the Arctic Circle than it is to Winnipeg. Churchill's economy is remarkably diverse for a town of its size. Many residents work in the town's port, loading grain and other products from railcars onto ships bound for Europe and elsewhere. The town's subarctic location has also attracted scientific enterprises, such as the Churchill Northern Studies Centre and the Institute of Arctic Ecophysiology. Churchill has also developed into a popular tourist spot where people can come to view polar bears in the wild.

Manitoba's northern country is exceedingly empty and remote. Only a dozen or so towns and Indian reserves exist in the top two-fifths of the province, and about half of these are

■ *Tourists flock to Manitoba for outdoor recreation and to see polar bears. Polar bear excursion trips are extremely popular.*

not connected by roads or rail—access is limited to those who can fly into the sites' tiny airfields.

The Aboriginal Population

The province's aboriginal population accounts for much of Manitoba's diversity, and dozens of tightly knit small communities abound, particularly in the central lake district. Some sixty First Nations tribal groups either are recognized by the state or are seeking recognition. They account for more than one hundred thousand provincial residents. Of those, 42 percent live in northern Manitoba and make up 57 percent of the population in that region. The tiny fly-in communities educate their children in their own schools, govern themselves with leaders selected from among them, and conduct their business of hunting, trapping, fishing, and mining.

The rest of the First Nations community lives in southern Manitoba, with 62 percent of those living in or around Winnipeg. Much smaller proportions of First Nations people live on reserves in the south. The vast majority of Manitoba's Métis live in the south, with more than half the population living in Winnipeg. Unemployment and lack of education continue to be problems among aboriginal peoples, with close to 20 percent of all employable Métis unemployed and about 30 percent of First Nations employable workers not holding jobs. Further, only slightly more than 33 percent of aboriginal youth age fifteen to twenty-nine have a high school diploma.

Despite these discouraging patterns, First Nations and Métis peoples are working diligently to overcome these hardships. A number of tribes have increasingly partnered with large companies, such as Manitoba Hydro, in developing energy and resource operations, thus giving needed income and jobs to native peoples.

A Focus on Education

While lifestyles differ from rural areas to cities, education is a key priority for all the people of Manitoba. More than two hundred thousand children attend public school in Manitoba, ranging from kindergarten through grade twelve. Another fifteen thousand or so attend independent schools, such as religious schools and French instruction schools. Since

■ *Members of First Nation tribal groups account for a large number of Manitoba's population.*

1970 Manitoba's public schools have offered French-only instruction to all who desire it.

Because so much of the province is made up of rural communities, the province provides extra support and money to rural schools, where class size, transportation, and other factors lead to higher-than-average costs. As a result, Manitoba has a reputation for a well-run school system. Elementary school children in Brandon, Fort la Bosse in southwestern Manitoba, and elsewhere, for instance, are connected to the Internet and provided up-to-date texts. In several southern towns, student-to-teacher ratios are as low as twelve-to-one.

In Winnipeg, students also enjoy access to technology, and they can often take advantage of more programs. One school classroom even has an individual Web site for each child, enabling children and their parents to access grades and class information using a password. Even in English-speaking schools, students may opt for a French-language immersion program that teaches all subjects in French. Ukrainian and Hebrew bilingual programs are offered in some schools, as well.

Aboriginal children can attend reserve schools or local public schools. Educators in both types of schools have begun in recent years to pay greater attention to instructing students on aboriginal culture. Schools have incorporated special texts and workbooks into the curriculum to enable students to understand history, social studies, and other subjects from a native perspective. Teachers in native and mainstream schools have increased their efforts to educate native children about their heritage, recognizing that many know little of their own history and culture.

Respected Colleges and Universities

Manitoba's emphasis on education extends beyond the twelfth grade. The province is home to three universities, a half-dozen colleges, and some 120 community college programs. The most prominent of these institutions is the University of Manitoba, which was founded in 1877 in Winnipeg. With more than twenty thousand full- and part-time students and twenty-two faculties and schools, it is one of the largest universities in Canada. The University of Manitoba is the province's most well-rounded institution, offering training in everything from linguistics and native studies to dentistry and medicine. Among the four U.M.-affiliated colleges that provide instruction in French is Le Collège Universitaire de St. Boniface, which offers excellent training in translation and languages and is a leader in producing bilingual professionals.

Students at the University of Winnipeg can choose among arts and sciences or study various aspects of Manitoba history, from Mennonite heritage to the history of Rupert's Land. Brandon University is a primarily undergraduate school with notable programs in education and music.

Every year thousands of Manitoba residents also take advantage of the many provincially funded community colleges. Red River College in Winnipeg offers numerous preparatory courses as well as training and certification in fields such as manufacturing technology, teaching, and business administration. In all, Manitoba universities award about six thousand degrees per year, and about one hundred thousand Manitoba residents have at least a bachelor's degree.

Art and Heritage

The widely varying lifestyles in Manitoba reflect in part the great diversity of the province's people. Overall, Manitobans enjoy good jobs and suitable housing, but disparities exist for native peoples and others not as fortunate. In addition, much of Manitoba is deeply connected to its heritage, with rural families still working the farms and native families hunting, trapping, and living by age-old methods. This deep connection to heritage ultimately shines in Manitobans' expression of art, music, dance, and culture.

Arts and Culture

The rich diversity of Manitoba is reflected in its range of artistic and cultural expression, from classical dance to folk festivals. Winnipeg is home to some of Canada's most renowned museums and institutions, and it remains the heart of cultural expression and cutting-edge contemporary work in the province. In addition, First Nations, Métis, Ukrainian, and other peoples actively celebrate their heritage in art that recalls connections to ancestors and the prairie, parkland, or woodland landscape. Manitoba also supports a growing film and television industry. Of course, with so much pristine wilderness, the people of Manitoba embrace outdoor activities from mountain biking to snowmobiling.

The Winnipeg Cultural Scene

The pearls of Manitoba's artistic expressions are generally produced and displayed in Winnipeg. The city offers a breadth of cultural attractions that draws visitors from the province, the country, and the world. The city is host to the Royal Winnipeg Ballet, the renowned Manitoba Museum of Man and Nature, an acclaimed orchestra, and the famed Winnipeg Art Gallery—the first civic art gallery in the nation.

Classical dance makes up one of the important cornerstones of the Winnipeg cultural scene. Begun in 1941, the Royal Winnipeg Ballet is the oldest ballet company in Canada and the longest continuously running company in North America. Recognizing its place in a diverse capital, it has premiered numerous ballets with varying cultural roots. It has performed to traditional Tchaikovsky and Bach dances but has also put on the French "Gaîté Parisienne," the Japanese "Butterfly," the native-based "Brave Song," and a Russian-style

■ *Dancers with the Royal Winnipeg Ballet rehearse. Classical dance is an important part of Winnipeg's artistic atmosphere.*

"Giselle." The Company performs one hundred times each season, and it has toured more than five hundred cities, winning accolades and distinction around the world. The Company also sponsors a renowned school that trains promising dancers.

Similar in classical nature to the ballet is the Winnipeg Symphony Orchestra. Like the Royal Winnipeg Ballet, its offerings are diverse. The orchestra is made up of a core of sixty-seven musicians with extra instrumentalists brought in as needed. The orchestra performs seventy-five times per season. Its most important innovation is the New Music Festival it hosts each year, which goes beyond classic orchestral pieces to include contemporary music. International artists often join the orchestra during the festival, and thousands attend in growing numbers each year. The orchestra also sponsors an educational outreach program for eleven thousand elementary school children in the southern Manitoba area. The children are treated to concerts that present music and dramatic scenes in English and French.

Aside from classical dance and music, Winnipeg hosts some of the most important historical and artistic works in the country. The renowned Manitoba Museum of Man and Nature is an important resource for students, historians, and scholars. It houses key exhibits in Manitoba's heritage. The Hudson's Bay Collection, for instance, contains more than ten thousand artifacts dating back to the early fur trade. Half of the exhibit is made up of First Nations, Métis, and Inuit artifacts that show how these various populations interacted with and adapted to the European fur traders. The province's natural heritage also plays a prominent role in the museum's offerings. The largest fossil of a trilobite, a distant extinct relative of scorpions and insects, was found in 1998 embedded in rock near Churchill in northern Manitoba and placed on display in the museum. The fossil is 445 million years old and measures twenty-eight inches (seventy-two centimeters) in length, almost a foot longer than the next-largest known specimen. The museum also houses a popular planetarium and a science center.

Founded in 1912, the Winnipeg Art Gallery was the nation's first civic gallery and remains the most prominent in the prairie provinces. The gallery is a cultural gathering place that houses eight exhibition rooms, a restaurant that overlooks a sculpture garden, a library, and meeting rooms and lecture halls. The twenty thousand pieces of art the Winnipeg Art Gallery holds range from sixteenth-century offerings to twentieth-century videos. The gallery places a special emphasis on Canadian and Manitoba artists, carrying works by and about renowned Manitoba artists such as Don Reichert, Esther Warkov, and Michael Olito. The gallery also has the largest collection of contemporary Inuit art in the world with more than ten thousand pieces, including sixty-seven hundred sculptures and more than one thousand drawings. A popular 1996 exhibition featured the work of Winnipeg-educated Inuit sculptor Manasie Akpaliapik.

■ Novelist Carol Shields

Carol Shields, Manitoba's most prominent novelist and author of the Pulitzer Prize-winning *The Stone Diaries,* was born in Chicago and grew up in Oak Park, Illinois. After completing her bachelor's degree at Hanover College in Indiana in the 1950s, she moved to Canada and obtained a master's at the University of Ottawa in Ontario. In 1980, she settled in Winnipeg and eventually became a professor and then chancellor at the University of Manitoba.

Her time in Manitoba has been fruitful. In 1987 her book *Swann* was nominated for the Governor-General's prize and was awarded the Arthur Ellis Award. Other books and awards followed, but no success was as great as that which came from *The Stone Diaries.* The 1993 novel was nominated for England's Booker Prize, and it won the Governor-General's Prize. In 1995, it won the Pulitzer Prize in the United States.

The story follows a woman who settles into a middle-class life as a wife and mother. Not extraordinary in plot, the book was lauded for its characterization and its understanding of women, memories, and personal growth. In some small way, the book may have roots in Shields herself. The author is married and the mother of five children. Now retired from academic life, she recently moved from Winnipeg to more temperate Victoria, British Columbia, to battle what has been diagnosed as a fatal case of breast cancer. In 2002 she released her newest novel, *Unless,* to critical acclaim.

From Winnie the Pooh to Neil Young

Manitoba's influence on popular culture includes a number of surprising cultural icons. The bear that inspired the creation of Winnie the Pooh was a black bear from Manitoba. Harry Coleburn, a soldier journeying across the country on his way to World War I, bought a black bear cub from a man who had shot the cub's mother. Coleburn named the bear Winnipeg, or Winnie for short, and, in England, he later gave the bear to a zoo. The bear was the favorite of A. Milne's son, Christopher Robin, and Christopher named his own teddy bear Winnie the Pooh. Milne later used the bear in his children's stories.

Winnipeg boasts two prominent magician/escape artists: Dean Gunnarson and the late Doug Henning. Gunnarson has dangled over Hoover Dam, opened for Aerosmith, and escaped a swamp full of crocodiles on

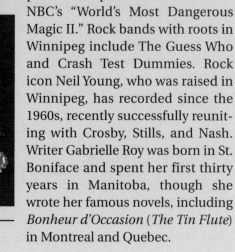

NBC's "World's Most Dangerous Magic II." Rock bands with roots in Winnipeg include The Guess Who and Crash Test Dummies. Rock icon Neil Young, who was raised in Winnipeg, has recorded since the 1960s, recently successfully reuniting with Crosby, Stills, and Nash. Writer Gabrielle Roy was born in St. Boniface and spent her first thirty years in Manitoba, though she wrote her famous novels, including *Bonheur d'Occasion* (*The Tin Flute*) in Montreal and Quebec.

■ *Musician Neil Young performs.*

The Winnipeg Art Gallery is also one of the few galleries in the province with a large photography collection.

A Network Connecting Artists

Art and culture that reflect the varied lifestyles and distinct character of the province can also be found outside Winnipeg. Since 1984 the Manitoba Arts Network has represented community arts councils and programming organizations throughout Manitoba. The network connects artists with communities and sponsors tours for theater performances, art shows, comedy acts, and musical performance artists. For small fees, community arts programs and galleries can join the Winnipeg-based organization and help bring in new and established artists and performers.

The Manitoba Arts Network has provided an important outlet for numerous artists. For example, family entertainer Jake Chenier is a French- and English-speaking singer and songwriter from the province. He has performed at numerous schools and community festivals, including the Winnipeg Children's Festival, and at cities such as The Pas, Flin Flon, and Thompson that are linked through the network. Similarly, David Hasselfield from the southwestern city of Deloraine has performed jazz and blues music across Canada and North America. Through the network he has appeared in Portage la Prairie and in other southern cities.

Rural artists frequently exhibit their work in small galleries and museums across the province. The Ukrainian-settled parkland town of Dauphin rotates exhibits in its art gallery every four to six weeks. Local artists such as Daniel Brown and Marilyn Park have displayed works that highlight the region's landscapes and wildlife. The gallery has also hosted the Manitoba Arts Network-sponsored Coastables, a traveling collection featuring artists from Manitoba and Saskatchewan. These pencil drawings, oil paintings, and other works often focus on the beauty and natural heritage of the province.

A Fledgling Film and Television Industry

Within recent years a small but growing film and television production industry has sprung up in Manitoba. A recent economic profile showed that the industry tripled in size from 1992 to 1998, at which time it had grown to a $60 million-per-year business that accounted for almost eight hundred jobs. Winnipeg may now rival Edmonton and Calgary as Canada's third-largest film-making center. (Toronto and Vancouver are firmly established in the top two spots.)

The growth of Manitoba's film industry has been due at least in part to support from the provincial government, which is actively courting filmmaking companies and encouraging video artists within the province. The province, through a special film and video tax credit, rebates to film companies 35 percent of the money paid to Manitoba residents working on film projects. It also funds Manitoba Film & Sound, a government corporation whose mission is to nurture and market the province's film and sound-recording industry. In addition, the nonprofit Manitoba Motion Picture Industries Association, which has over one thousand producers, directors, writers, and other members, promotes the film industry in Manitoba. For example, it connects interested workers and students with practical training programs that can help individuals get started in careers in film.

Manitoba is in the process of gaining a major new filmmaking facility with the construction of the spacious Prairie Production Centre in Winnipeg. The first phase of the project, a state-of-the-art, all-season, fifteen thousand-square-foot studio, is complete. Plans are in the works for the second phase, which would include an office complex for post-production and film industry tenants. The $7.7 million facility, the first of its kind in Manitoba, has been funded by a private partnership as well as by contributions from the governments of Manitoba and Canada.

Manitoba's efforts to boost its film industry profile have paid off with increasing numbers of television series, documentaries, feature films, and special effects being shot in the province. For example, a Winnipeg-based special effects company, Frantic Films, has recently worked on scenes for Hollywood films including *Storm of the Century* and *Swordfish*. Business leaders and government officials in Manitoba agree that the investment is well worth the opportunity to develop a bustling industry and to help expose the province to outsiders.

A Vibrant Festival Scene

Manitoba loves to celebrate its history and diversity through festivals and city-wide celebrations. Perhaps the most popular annual festival in Manitoba is Winnipeg's Folklorama, which now attracts more than four hundred thousand visitors each August. The two-week multicultural extravaganza was begun in 1970 as a celebration of Manitoba's one hundredth birthday. Folklorama features dozens of pavilions, each representing a culture from around the world, scattered throughout the city. The pavilions sell ethnic foods, exhibit interesting cultural displays, and host nightly concerts, native dances, and other performances.

But Folklorama is hardly the only Winnipeg festival honoring the diversity and heritage of the province. The Festival du Voyageur, held each February in St. Boniface, is the largest winter festival in Canada. It commemorates the "voyageurs," the adventurous seventeenth- and eighteenth-century French fur traders who traversed the continent in canoes. The event opens with ceremonies in heated pavilions, including one at a reconstructed aboriginal camp and another at Fort Gibraltar.

The North West Company built the original Fort Gibraltar in 1809, during the height of its rivalry with the Hudson's Bay Company and not far from its Fort Douglas. Gibraltar lasted only seven years before Hudson's Bay Company forces captured and destroyed it. British authorities admitted that the destruction was illegal and allowed the North West Company to rebuild Gibraltar the following year. It lasted until 1852, when a Red River flood washed it away. In 1978 the Festival du Voyageur rebuilt the log-palisaded fort, initially just for the winter festival but recently, with the addition of a replica of the Governor's House, as a year-round historic attraction.

The ten-day Festival du Voyageur features a fur-trade-era costume ball, sled dog races, ice sculptures, slides, and mazes. Trading posts offer arts and crafts, foods, and memorabilia of the Scottish, French, Métis, and native cultures that dominated the fur trade era. The festival is hosted by two thousand volunteers and eighty community organizations and has welcomed as many as one hundred and fifty thousand people.

■ *During one of Manitoba's many festivals, men row a York Boat in a historic reenactment.*

Winnipeg is also host to a handful of smaller festivals that bring art, music, and entertainment to the big city. Each July, thousands gather in Birds Hill Park for the Winnipeg Folk Festival, a draw for music lovers from across the province. The show has brought in Manitoba performers such as children's songwriter and storyteller Sheldon Oberman, folk group Easily Amused, and the native Cree, Ojibway, Assiniboine, and Sioux dance group Summer Bear Dance Troupe. Other artists from around the continent make the trip as well. Similarly, the Winnipeg Writers' Festival attracts top writers who instruct on their trade and help others make connections in the industry. Among those who have been featured in the past are novelist Sandra Birdsell, who was born and raised in Manitoba, and Broken Songs, a collaboration between poet Margaret Sweatman and jazz musician Glenn Buhr. Finally, the International Children's Festival held in The Forks National Historic Site provides frolicsome live entertainment.

Rural and Native Cultural Celebrations

Manitoba's many small towns and native reserves also offer an array of cultural displays and festivities to express their heritage. The events typically happen on a smaller scale than what is offered in Winnipeg, but the rural celebrations nevertheless unite communities and bind friends and families.

At the southern tip of Lake Winnipeg, Selkirk (population ten thousand) hosts the Triple S Fair and Rodeo, now in its 125th year. The July event combines all of the elements of great rodeo, such as saddle bronc riding, steer wrestling, calf roping, and bull riding, with the attractions of a large country fair. Triple S also includes live entertainment, a cattle show, auto and truck displays, and handicrafts and homemaking exhibits. The event is a chance for thousands to experience the province's western heritage.

Even on a much smaller scale, towns' heritage and culture are at the center of annual celebrations. In the parkland town of Minitonas, north of Duck Mountain Provincial Park, the population of barely one thousand is proud to celebrate its

■ *Native North Americans prepare for a pageant of canoes. Native celebrations make up a large part of Manitoba's cultural festivities.*

■ The Icelandic Festival in Gimli

Located on the southwestern shore of Lake Winnipeg, Gimli was first settled in 1875 by immigrants from Iceland. In Norse mythology, Gimli means *paradise*, which describes the area during the summer if you like gorgeous lakefront beaches and plenty of opportunity to swim, sail, sunbathe, and boat. During subsequent periods of immigration Gimli welcomed influxes of Hungarian, German, Polish, and Ukrainian settlers, but the town has never lost its Icelandic pride. That pride is best displayed during Íslendingadagurinn, the Icelandic festival that has been held in Gimli every August since 1933 (the festival started in 1890 in Winnipeg). Gimli is the "Icelandic Capital" of Manitoba, which has the world's largest concentration of people with Icelandic ancestry outside of Iceland, and the festival is renowned not only in Manitoba but also back in Iceland.

A highlight of the weekend festival is the parade with participants and folk dancers dressed in vintage costumes like the black-vested and silver-decorated "upphlutur." The festival also typically features musical acts like the Arborg children's choir, Viking boat races, and booths where visitors can taste traditional Icelandic-Canadian foods like síld (herring) and vinarterta (a baked dessert). The festival often attracts major political figures from Manitoba and Iceland as well as Icelandic celebrities like Magnus ver Magnusson, four-time winner of the "World's Strongest Man" title.

ethnic diversity. The residents are a mix of Anglo-Saxons, Germans, Slavs, and Ukrainians, most of whom still work in agriculture or forestry. Minitonas hosts a fruit festival in September, and it invites residents downtown every December for the annual Christmas party.

In a similar way, First Nations peoples draw together as communities with a common heritage through competitions and powwows, traditional celebrations that generally include singing, dance contests, and tribal leadership speeches. Powwows are typically held by individual tribes across the province.

In July 2002, First Nation, Native American, Inuit, and Métis participants came together in Winnipeg for the fifth North American Indigenous Games (NAIG). The event, first held in Edmonton in 1990, drew more than seven thousand aboriginal participants in six age groups, from bantam (thirteen and fourteen years old) to masters (fifty years and older). They competed in sixteen sports, including the native sports archery, canoeing, and lacrosse as well as conventional sports such as basketball, boxing, and soccer. With financial support from the governments of Winnipeg and Manitoba, as well as corporations, the NAIG entertained and educated athletes and visitors. "These games are a way of life that has been laid out by our ancestors," noted NAIG council president Alex Nelson. "Sport encompassed completely the emotional, mental, physical, and spiritual part of one's self. We are only re-awakening what has been laid down before."[13]

Outdoor Recreation in the Parks

With so much striking wilderness, Manitoba is an ideal location for all types of outdoor activities. Manitoba's two national parks are Riding Mountain and Wapusk, the latter of which is south of Churchill and the home to one of the world's largest denning sites for polar bears. Manitoba is also working with the Canadian government to establish a new Manitoba Lowlands National Park in the Interlake area around Grand Rapids. The province has more than one hundred provincial park areas, the largest being Sand Lakes in the far north. It is one of four huge new provincial parks the province established during the 1990s, in effect doubling the total provincial park area.

Among the most popular provincial parks for wilderness activities are Whiteshell, east of Winnipeg on the border of Ontario, and Clearwater Lake, just north of The Pas. Clearwater harbors trophy-size lake trout and northern pike and attracts motor, sail, and paddle boaters. Winter in the park is perfect for ice fishing, cross-country skiing, and snowmobiling. Farther north, near Thompson, Paint Lake Provincial Park embodies the rugged beauty of the Canadian Shield. Visitors come to see the lake's unique islands, enjoy the beaches, fish for walleye and pike, or hike around the terrain.

Less than an hour's drive north of Winnipeg is Grand Beach Provincial Park, which features a two-mile-long (three-kilometer) stretch of white sand on the southernmost tip of Lake Winnipeg. The beach has been hailed as one of the world's finest, and it can easily attract up to twenty thousand people

■ *Outdoor activities such as fishing are a popular pastime for many Manitobans.*

a day during stretches of the summer. The shallow water with numerous sandbars is moderately warm, making for good swimming. On the east beach, visitors can camp near huge sand dunes and enjoy a quieter atmosphere than that associated with the vendors and restaurants of the west beach.

Raw nature contrasts with turn-of-the-century dam technology at Pinawa Dam Provincial Park. The dam, located on the Winnipeg River south of Lake Winnipeg, was built in 1906 and was the province's first hydroelectric generating station. The dam was closed in 1951 so that the river could flow unimpeded to the new Seven Sisters Hydro Station downstream. Volunteers and provincial officials turned Pinawa Dam into an attraction by building an amphitheater, installing interpretative signs, and building a walking bridge and nature trail.

Duck Mountain Provincial Park is a favorite for nature lovers. It comprises rolling terrain, valley meadows, woodlands, and wetlands, and it encompasses numerous spring-fed, deep-blue glacial lakes. It is home to various plant and tree species as well as black bear, moose, and deer. Careful listeners may catch the bugling of bull elk. The park is also a favorite for dayhikers. Pine Meadow Trail brings hikers into view of one of the oldest pine trees in the province, while walkers along Valley River Trail can view a tepee site. Dedicated hikers and campers can take trails that explore rougher country in the mountains. Many Manitoba residents consider Duck Mountain an ideal place to escape city life and connect with nature.

The Red River Corridor

Manitoba's many wilderness parks meet the desires of those who want anything from ice climbing to windsurfing. For those who prefer historical and cultural attractions, the so-called "Red River Corridor" in the area of Winnipeg offers plenty. At the southern tip of Winnipeg is St. Norbert Provincial Park, a heritage site illustrating Métis family life circa the late 1800s. Visitors can find a depiction of a French-Canadian agricultural community and a straw-and-mud Red River frame house.

In Winnipeg, tourists and residents alike congregate at The Forks. The meeting point of the Red and Assiniboine Rivers, The Forks is now a National Historic Site and a bustling urban scene. "A decade of restoration work," notes *Canada Coast to Coast*, "has transformed a one-time district of bleak, century-old railway yards at the junction of the Red and Assiniboine rivers into one of the city's most popular

■ *The main courtyard of the Forks Shopping Centre attracts many visitors. The Forks area of Manitoba is a popular place for tourists to congregate.*

gathering places."[14] Citizens and visitors flock to The Forks for river cruises, a picturesque riverside trail, a market in renovated stables, and Canada's largest children's museum.

A few blocks' walk from The Forks, visitors can enter a small, charming park through a massive stone gateway. It is all that remains of Upper Fort Garry, the Hudson's Bay Company's administrative center for the area during most of the nineteenth century. For a vivid experience of life in nineteenth-century Hudson's Bay Company fort, a short distance away in the northern end of town visitors can find restored Lower Fort Garry. The Hudson's Bay Company built Lower Garry beginning in the 1840s because its higher-ground siting made it less vulnerable than the Upper Fort to the frequent floods of the Red and Assiniboine. Lower Garry Fort National Historic Site is the oldest stone fur-trading post still intact in North America as well as the largest group of original nineteenth-century fur-trade buildings in Canada. Costumed interpreters and numerous exhibits at the stone-walled fort help commemorate not only the fur trade but also the company's history of agricultural and industrial shipping.

History and Heritage

Manitoba's rich history and its natural beauty are prominent elements of its self-identity. The people are proud of their heritage and go out of their way to celebrate the province's ethnic diversity. This cultural pride and respect for the land, however, can also factor in the difficult political and economic choices that ultimately will decide Manitoba's future.

Current Challenges

T he multicultural and urban/rural nature of Manitoba can be the source of great strength, yet it can also point to some of Manitoba's greatest challenges. While the federal and provincial governments have granted a degree of self-government to the First Nations, many still suffer from staggering rates of poverty, unemployment, and lack of education. Economic challenges, however, are not limited to First Nations peoples. Manitoba is trying to expand its business base and increase its population, in part because population and economic growth have been only moderate over the last decade, while health care costs have soared and new security costs pose a threat to the economy. The province now faces a crucial period as it struggles to gain financial strength and provide adequately for its citizens in the face of fluctuating world economies.

First Nations Struggle to Thrive

Manitoba's economy has been slow to filter benefits down to one of the groups in greatest need: the aboriginal peoples. The lack of money and jobs leads directly to lower-than-average life expectancies and higher rates of disease. While all aboriginal peoples lag behind in most social indicators, those living on reserves have struggled the most. While aboriginal male life expectancy is only two years behind the national average in urban areas, it is ten years behind on reserves. On a similar note, infant mortality is three times higher among aboriginal populations than among nonnative populations, and most of the deaths occur more than twenty-eight days

■ *Cree Indians gather to chop wood in a Cree Indian camp. Aboriginal people living on reserves struggle to survive.*

after birth—meaning many aboriginal children die after they have left urban hospitals and returned to isolated areas.

Unemployment for aboriginal peoples is nearly as discouraging, both for natives living in urban areas and for those on the reserves. On the whole, the First Nations unemployment rate hovers around 30 percent, more than three times higher than the rate among non-aboriginals. The Métis tend to face a better job market with labor participation rates similar to non-aboriginals, although their unemployment rate is still a high 20 percent. Consequently, aboriginals as a whole have a lower standard of living, less access to health care, and less connection to the mainstream economy than non-aboriginals.

The dire circumstances among aboriginals remain in spite of federal funding targeted to boost their income and employment. Critics of tribal governments charge that the money spent on aboriginal peoples is not being distributed properly, with tribal chiefs and their inner circle being the main beneficiaries. Former Manitoba politician Jean Allard believes the answer to that problem is to have the federal government devote some of the transfer payments—perhaps $400 per person—directly to individuals. Others believe that the main problem is geographical: many of the reserves are in remote areas, essentially cut off from the best technology, health care, and businesses. Another potential fundamental problem is the lack of access to high-quality education.

Improving Aboriginal Education

Only half of Manitoba's aboriginal adults ages thirty to thirty-nine have graduated from high school, compared with the non-aboriginal rate of more than 75 percent. Further, reserve high school graduation rates are even lower—about 40 percent compared with more than 50 percent for off-reserve First Nations and nearly 60 percent for Métis peoples. Again, isolation seems to play a major role: of the fifteen First Nations communities that have the highest rates of adults failing to complete ninth grade, eleven were accessible only by air. Postsecondary education rates among aboriginals are also low. The number of aboriginals obtaining some university education or a degree is half that of non-aboriginals.

The situation has inspired concerned people within the province to lobby for change. The province is funding the building of more schools on the reserves. A number of reserves are using "interventions"—coordinated efforts by parents, teachers, administrators, and community members to help those who appear on the verge of dropping out of school. Manitoba's colleges and universities have begun to increase the number of instructors and assistants with training in aboriginal affairs. For example, the University of Winnipeg now offers an Aboriginal Educational Assistant program. The program offers aboriginals instruction on First Nations culture, educational issues, and Canadian school law and trains the individuals to work as educational assistants in classrooms across the province.

Other programs assist aboriginals' transition from high school to university. The University of Manitoba, for instance, places poverty-stricken students in counselor-supported networks and classes. Eighty-five percent of the program's participants are aboriginal. Further, the university sponsors an aboriginal student center that provides support for the academic, cultural, physical, and personal needs of aboriginal students. Similarly creative approaches are needed for Manitoba's other challenges.

Expanding Manitoba's Economy

During Canada's westward expansion, Manitoba was an economic and agricultural power. Today, however, the province's economy ranks behind the industrial provinces (Ontario, Quebec) and the resource-rich west (Alberta, British Columbia) and ahead of only the severely depressed maritime provinces. The post-2001 slowdown in the global economy further threatens the overall economic vitality of the province and its efforts to diversify and grow. The provincial government is investing in education, adjusting taxes, and using other measures to try to attract knowledge-based and high-tech industries.

■ The Plight of the Family Farm

While much of southern Manitoba remains rural and centered around farming communities, the family grain farm is increasingly threatened. Indeed, this may be one of the bleakest times in the province's history for family-owned farms.

The grain industry prospered during the early and middle 1990s when grain-importing countries like Russia were purchasing large supplies to supplement local shortages. In recent years, however, the demand for grain has slackened, and prices have fallen. The low prices and the relatively low government subsidies have threatened family farms across Manitoba. To stay profitable, farmers must farm larger and larger amounts of land and invest in increasingly expensive equipment and fuel. Manitoba's twenty-four thousand farms (down by 5 percent from 1991) now average 776 acres (314 hectares), compared to 479 acres (194 hectares) in 1966. The survivors in this difficult cycle tend to be agribusiness companies that buy small family farms and combine them into super-farms. As more and more farming families are bought out and young people leave for higher-paying jobs in the city, farming communities begin to suffer a slow death. Many of Manitoba's farming towns now have half the population they had in 1960.

For its part, the Manitoba government has responded with several initiatives. It continues to lobby the federal government for more farm subsidies, though such lobbying has not always proven successful. It has cut farm property taxes, increased alternative-energy incentives, and developed a program to improve drainage and watershed management. Even so, the long-term trend toward agribusiness super-farms may be too much for the provincial government to overcome on its own.

From 1996 to 2001, Manitoba's population grew by less than 1 percent, suggesting in part that the province has failed to establish a robust economy that could attract new residents. Economic analysts foresee further weakness in resource sectors such as forestry and mining because of a drop in prices around the world. The terrorist attacks of September 11, 2001, in the United States further damaged consumer confidence and caused a dramatic slowdown in tourism. Manitoba businesses have had to spend more on border security, security at major industry and government centers, first-response health care coordination, and airport and mail-handling safety. Concurrently, exports to the United States have been hurt by the sluggish American economy.

Manitoba is responding to these economic challenges with various measures. To spur overall growth in the economy, in 1999 the provincial government led by Premier Gary Doer began to reduce personal and property taxes every year. The tax relief helped Manitoba become one of only four provinces where, according to a recent study, residents' disposable income was expected to rise in 2002. Manitoba's government has also coordinated its efforts with industries'. For example, high oil prices and instability in oil markets in recent years have inspired government and industry investment in alternative forms of energy and fuel. Manitoba Hydro and other utilities are investing in alternative fuel sources like ethanol, wind, biomass, geothermal heat, and hydrogen. The biotechnology and food sectors are also seeing further investment and growth. The federal and provincial governments are pressing forward with plans to build a $25 million Center for Nutraceutical and Functional Foods Research at the University of Manitoba. The Center will draw on health, food, and biotechnology resources from across the province.

Private industry is also moving forward on its own in the face of the economic challenges. J. R. Simplot Company, an agribusiness corporation, is building a new $120 million potato processing plant in Portage la Prairie. The chemical manufacturing company Albchem Industries is putting the finishing touches on a $40 million sodium chlorate (a chemical used to bleach paper) plant in the southwestern town of Virden. Standard Aero, an aircraft engine and accessory repair and overhaul company, is expanding its Manitoba operation, as is manufacturer Canada West Foods. Maple Leaf Meats recently completed a major hog processing plant in Brandon.

■ *Researchers work in a lab in Manitoba. The provincial government is trying to attract knowledge-based industries to expand the economy.*

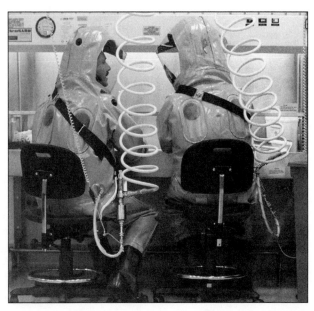

Strengthening Education

Manitoba's government and the private sector are also teaming up to strengthen the province's educational system. Both see postsecondary education, in particular, as a key factor in developing the skilled workers needed to attract more industries to the province. The province recently committed extra money and resources to creating new spaces and programs in its public colleges and universities. The result has been a 12 percent increase in enrollment at those institutions.

Private citizens are deeply involved in the efforts, as well. Government investment of $50 million at the University of Manitoba, for example, has been matched by private donors. The university is pressing forward with a $100 million campus building initiative designed to broaden the university's scope and increase its enrollment.

Manitoba is also expanding its efforts to reach various groups with improved education and training opportunities. For example, the province and local industries have launched an apprenticeship program that will increase nursing training opportunities. Another program offers aboriginal students training in hydro development. Further, the government is looking to improve the administration of adult education programs, and it is expanding access to college education in northern communities.

The High Cost of Health Care

As is the case across Canada, soaring health care costs are a growing concern. Manitoba participates in the federal government's universal health care plan, receiving federal payments to subsidize access to basic services. Manitoba tends to spend more money per capita on health care than most of the other provinces, and the soaring costs are outstripping the provincial government's ability to provide services. In recent years, pharmaceutical costs have been increasing by 15 to 20 percent every year, far outpacing the rate of federal funding. Manitoba is also facing a critical shortage in nurses and other health care professionals.

Lately, Manitoba has responded to its ongoing health care crisis by investing heavily in preventive care. It has opened new Community Health Access Centers in two Winnipeg locations, and it has provided grants to more than one hundred medical students who were willing to set up practices in widespread Manitoba communities. The government and industry have been studying workplace injuries, and new laws are being passed aimed at reducing those injuries. The government has expanded its mosquito control services to re-

■ Nurses Wanted

Manitoba's desperate shortage of nurses is at least partly the result of decisions made by the provincial government in the early 1990s. It sought to rein in health care costs by streamlining the profession. Hundreds of nursing positions were either abolished or simply left unfilled. The glut of qualified nurses led to fewer men and women enrolling in nurse training programs. Many trained nurses migrated south to the United States, where nursing jobs were plentiful. The nurses who remained faced difficult working conditions. Many were forced to cut back from full- to part-time employment, with their benefits being reduced accordingly. In addition, nurses faced an increased patient and administrative load with fewer nursing assistants and hospital staff persons for support.

Today, the province is looking for other ways to reform health care. It has sought to address the shortage in nurses by reinstating the nursing diploma at the University of Manitoba and increasing nurses' salaries. Although nurses are back in demand in Manitoba, the job market has been slow to respond, and the shortage continues.

duce certain infectious diseases, and a new Drinking Water Office is administering new guidelines to drinking water facility operators.

Although such initiatives have led to progress, health care remains a growing concern that threatens to erupt into a full-scale crisis. Manitoba is not currently considering policies, like those being pursued in Alberta, aimed at privatizing many health care services and requiring patients to make extensive out-of-pocket payments. But with costs rising and the means to control them limited, the future for Manitoba health care seems uncertain.

Land Claims and Resource Management

Another ongoing issue for Manitoba relates to land claim and resource-sharing challenges from aboriginal groups. Recent Supreme Court of Canada decisions have given merit to the native position that oral agreements and other concessions made by earlier Canadian governments were not being honored. Thus, native groups including many in Manitoba have sought access to or control of disputed lands as well as restitution for revenues made from resources on those lands.

Land claims are particularly important in northern Manitoba, where a number of tribes are disputing the census data taken at the time of the original treaties. In the treaties signed by First Nations and Canada between 1871 and 1910, land was apportioned by the number of members in each tribe. (Each family of five persons was to be provided with 160 to 640 acres of land.) But many northern First Nations bands were either drastically undercounted or were left out of the treaty process altogether, meaning that they received little to no land. In recent years, the two sides have sought to rectify the century-long dispute. In 1997, Canada, Manitoba, and twenty First Nations signed the Manitoba Treaty Land Entitlement Framework Agreement, which is intended to select, acquire, and transfer land to the tribes.

The Framework Agreement provides more than seventeen thousand square miles (forty-four hundred square kilometers) of land to the First Nations. Almost one-third of that land is being handed over by the provincial government as it settles with each band. The federal government further set aside $76 million so that First Nations bands with little or no provincial-owned land nearby can purchase private land to

■ *Manitoba's Southern Chiefs Organization leads a protest outside Winnipeg Stadium, claiming unfair treatment by the province's government.*

meet the amount set by the agreement. Agreements with individual bands must be ratified by the separate communities, so the process as a whole is quite lengthy and is expected to take several years. Still, the provincial government credits the agreement with accelerating the settlement of land claims.

Even beyond these measures, difficult issues remain to be negotiated between the government and the First Nations. Some land that had previously been set aside as federal land for mineral exploitation or power development now borders on or is part of First Nations land. The presence of natural resources, however, can be a boon to First Nations groups by providing jobs and money. Manitoba is working to develop land and resource comanagement deals with both First Nations and Métis groups. For example, an agreement between Manitoba Hydro and the First Nations of Split Lake and Nelson House (both are Cree bands) provides for training programs that eventually can place First Nations workers in high-paying jobs within Manitoba Hydro. The provincial government views the agreement as a model to follow in developing agreements with other aboriginal groups.

Natural Resources and the Environment

Manitoba's lush forests and uninhabited swamplands are home to numerous important species, but they also attract the attention of industries vital to the economic health of the province. These industries face mounting difficulties, both from environmental challenges and from foreign competitors. In Manitoba, timber companies are bound by the government's Forest Management Plan, which seeks to provide a steady flow of wood products as well as a quick replenishing of forest stripped for lumber. Companies must undertake environmental studies before cutting any trees. They must also guarantee that new trees are successfully planted in lumbered areas to replenish the forests. Similarly, Manitoba Hydro must assess the environmental impact of any plan to develop a river as a source of power.

A number of environmental groups argue, however, that Manitoba doesn't do enough to safeguard its wilderness. Old-growth forests in particular, they note, cannot be easily replaced after logging operations simply by planting trees. First Nations bands have filed lawsuits against Manitoba Hydro, saying that the company's operations have polluted or muddied rural drinking water. For its part, Manitoba is expanding

Manitoba Hydro's conservation mandate. The provincial government is also setting aside wetland and forest areas that will not be used for development.

Economic problems are not easily resolved, either. The forest industry has been victimized by falling world prices. As part of an ongoing trade dispute, the United States in 2002 threatened to impose new tariffs against Canadian lumber, including lumber from Manitoba. Such trade restrictions would further weaken Manitoba's forestry industry. The Canadian government is looking to the international courts for help, but for now, the challenge to the industry remains.

■ Manitoba Hydro Under Fire

Tensions between Manitoba Hydro and its critics reached new levels in the first years of the new millennia. Environmentalists say that flooding caused by Manitoba Hydro dams destroys the shoreline vegetation that many species depend on for food. In addition, critics say the various dams and diversions lead to massive soil erosion along rivers that causes harm to many plant and animal species. Beyond that, the erosion leads to muddy water, necessitating the use of potent chemicals to convert it to drinking water.

Perhaps more serious, say critics, are the consequences for people. Aboriginal groups claim that Manitoba Hydro has not lived up to the 1977 Northern Flood Agreement, made to compensate tribes adversely affected by northern dams. Several tribes claim that dams have harmed hunting and fishing so thoroughly that reservation economies have been harmed irreparably.

One of the bitterest disputes is between the Pimicikamak Cree Nation of Cross Lake, south of Thompson, and Manitoba Hydro. The band holds Manitoba Hydro responsible for the deaths of fifty members, who, according to the Pimicikamaks, were killed either directly or indirectly by the massive hydro projects nearby. In 2001, Manitoba Hydro filed a $1.2 million lawsuit against the Pimicikamak Cree, alleging that the tribe had failed to pay its electric bills. A $100 million countersuit by the tribe said that the company had thoroughly contaminated drinking water. The tribe also contended that it refused to pay its bills because the power company would not live up to the Northern Flood Agreement.

For its part, Manitoba Hydro claims it offers an important service to surrounding communities and the province by providing low-cost power with a renewable resource. Further, agreements between the company and aboriginal groups provide for jobs and training for many aboriginals. Despite such assurances of good will, the wrangling and tensions seem likely to continue.

Working Collectively Toward Solutions

Because of its central location in Canada, Manitoba has long been an important link between eastern and western parts of the country, from its early days on the fur trade route to its current position as a major rail and road link in the shipment of wheat and other goods. This keystone position has also led to Manitoba becoming the most culturally diverse of Canada's provinces, including major representation among English, French, German, Ukrainian, Métis, and First Nations peoples. Lacking the rich energy/forestry natural resources of Alberta and British Columbia and less successful than neighboring Ontario at drawing new industries, Manitoba today is struggling to diversify its economy and establish an identity that encompasses its diverse heritage. There are few easy solutions, but the province has taken steps to address its problems. Many of its citizens do so with a willingness to coordinate their efforts with others and a commitment to broaden the opportunities for all of Manitoba's peoples.

■ *Winnipeg, Manitoba, faces many challenges in its future, but it will continue to thrive as it has done for many years.*

Facts About Manitoba

Government

- Form: Parliamentary system with federal and provincial levels
- Highest official: Premier, who administers provincial legislation and regulations
- Capital: Winnipeg
- Entered confederation: July 15, 1870 (fifth of the provinces)
- Provincial flag: Red Ensign, with a solid red background, British Union Jack in upper left, provincial shield with plains bison in right-center
- Motto: "Glorious and free"

Land

- Area: 250,999 square miles (650,087 square kilometers); 6.5% of total land of Canada; sixth-largest province; rivers and lakes cover approximately 16% of Manitoba's territory
- Boundaries: bounded on the north by Hudson Bay and Nunavut, on the west by Saskatchewan, on the south by North Dakota and Minnesota, and on the east by Ontario
- Bordering bodies of water: Hudson Bay to the northeast
- National parks: Riding Mountain, Wapusk
- Provincial parks: 106, encompassing approximately 11,500 square miles (30,000 square kilometers); the largest is Sand Lakes in the north

- Highest point: Baldy Mountain, 2,730 feet (832 meters)
- Largest lake: Lake Winnipeg, 9,417 square miles (24,390 square kilometers); sixth-largest freshwater lake in Canada and fourteenth-largest in world
- Other major lakes: Winnipegosis, Manitoba, Cedar, Southern Indian, Cross, Island, Gods
- Longest river: Nelson, 400 miles (644 kilometers)
- Other major rivers: Red, Assiniboine, Hayes, Churchill, Winnipeg
- Time zones: Central Standard Time
- Geographical extremes: 49° N to 60° N latitude; 102° W to 89° W longitude

Climate

- Lowest recorded temperature, Winnipeg: −49° F (−45° C), Feb. 18, 1966
- Longest skin-freezing windchill: 170 hours, Jan. 24, 1966 (Canadian record)

People

- Population: 1,119,583 (2001 census); fifth-highest population of provinces and territories; 3.7% of Canada's total population of 30,007,094
- Annual growth rate: 0.5% from 1996 to 2001 (seventh-highest growth rate among provinces and territories)
- Density: 2.1 persons per square kilometer (Canadian national average: 3)
- Location: 72% urban; 28% rural; 60% of Manitoba residents live in the Winnipeg metropolitan area
- Predominant heritages: British, French, Métis, aboriginal
- Largest ethnic groups: German, Ukrainian, Filipino, Polish, Dutch, Chinese, South Asian, Icelandic
- Major religious groups: Catholic, Protestant, Jewish
- Primary languages (first learned and still understood): 80% English, 6% German, 5% French, and 9% other languages, led by Ukrainian, Cree, Tagalog (Filipino), and Polish

- Largest metropolitan areas: Winnipeg, population 671,274, an increase of 0.6% between 1996 and 2001; eighth-largest metropolitan area in Canada
- Other major cities: Brandon, Portage la Prairie, Thompson, Selkirk
- Life expectancy at birth, 3-year average 1995–1997: Men 75.2 years; women 80.5; total both sexes 77.9, tied for sixth among provinces and territories (Canadian average: men 75.4; women 81.2; total 78.4)
- Immigration 7/1/2000-6/30/2001:4,805, 1.9% of Canadian total of 252,088; fifth-highest of provinces and territories
- Births 7/1/2000-6/30/2001: 14,170
- Deaths 7/1/2000-6/30/2001: 10,304
- Marriages in 1998: 6,218
- Divorces in 1998: 2,443

Plants and Animals

- Provincial bird: Great gray owl
- Provincial flower: Prairie crocus
- Provincial tree: White spruce
- Endangered, threatened, or vulnerable species: 20, including western prairie fringed orchid, western silvery aster, burrowing owl, peregrine falcon, piping plover, whooping crane, great plains toad, mule deer

Holidays

- National: January 1 (New Year's Day); Good Friday; Easter; Easter Monday; Monday preceding May 25 (Victoria or Dollard Day); July 1 or, if this date falls on a Sunday, July 2 (Canada's birthday); 1st Monday of September (Labour Day); 2nd Monday of October (Thanksgiving); November 11 (Remembrance Day); December 25 (Christmas); December 26 (Boxing Day)
- Provincial: None

Economy

- Gross domestic product per capita: $25,328 in 1999, ninth among provinces and territories and 74.9% compared to U.S. average[15]

- Gross provincial product: $32.8 billion at market prices in 2000, fifth among the provinces and territories and 3.2% of gross national product

- Major exports: grains, minerals, machinery

- Agriculture: wheat, canola, flaxseed, barley, oats, rye, sunflower seeds, buckwheat, field peas, potatoes, livestock (beef, dairy, hogs)

- Tourism: sightseeing, hiking, boating, windsurfing, recreational fishing

- Logging: pulp, paper, lumber

- Manufacturing: food products, machinery, metals, transportation equipment

- Mining: nickel, copper, zinc, gold, cadmium, silver, limestone, granite, clay, bentonite

Notes

Chapter 1 : From the Prairies to the Bay

1. Gerald Friesen, *The Canadian Prairies: A History.* Lincoln: University of Nebraska Press, 1984, p. 6.
2. Quoted in "Provincial Bird: Great Gray Owl," *Manitoba Geobopological Survey.* www.geobop.com.

Chapter 2 : The First Nations, the Europeans, and the Métis

3. Marcel Giraud, *The Métis in the Canadian West,* Volume I. London, England, and Lincoln, NB: University of Alberta Press, 1986, p. 433.
4. Friesen, *The Canadian Prairies,* p. 79.
5. Quoted in "Battle of Seven Oaks," *Angelhair's Home Page.* www.geocities.com.
6. Friesen, *The Canadian Prairies,* p. 97.

Chapter 3 : Immigrants Shape the Province

7. Friesen, *The Canadian Prairies,* p. 195.
8. Ronald A. Wells, ed., *Letters from a Young Emigrant in Manitoba.* Winnipeg: University of Manitoba, 1981, pp. 111–12.
9. Pierre Berton, *The Promised Land.* Toronto: McClelland and Stewart, 1984, p. 15.
10. Quoted in Bruce Cherney, "Ukrainian Immigration," *R.F. Morrison School.* http://home.merlin.mb.ca.
11. Cherney, "Ukrainian Immigration."

Chapter 4 : Life in Manitoba Today

12. "The Exchange District," *Exchange District.*
    www.exchangedistrict.org.

Chapter 5 : Arts and Culture

13. Quoted in "Changing the Future of Games," *North American Indigenous Games.* www.2002naig.com.

14. Andrew R. Byers, ed., *Canada Coast to Coast.* Montreal: Reader's Digest Association (Canada), 1998, p. 95.

Facts About Manitoba

15. "Canada: Regional Gross Domestic Product Data: 1999," *Demographia.* www.demographia.com.

Chronology

ca. 11000 B.C. Nomadic hunters filter into the grasslands of present-day Manitoba from the west.

ca. 5000 B.C. Woodland tribes develop in forested regions of Canadian Shield.

ca. 500 B.C. First Nations develop trade in copper and flint with tribes from Great Lakes and other regions.

Early 1600s The Chipewyan in the northern wooded areas, the Cree in the central forests, and the Assiniboine in the south are the main tribes of present-day Manitoba.

1612 British captain Thomas Button lands two ships near the mouth of the Nelson and Hayes Rivers, becoming the first European to visit the region.

1670 King Charles II of England grants control over "Rupert's Land," immense area surrounding Hudson Bay, to Hudson's Bay Company.

1684 The Hudson's Bay Company establishes the first York Factory trading post at the mouth of the Hayes and Nelson Rivers.

1688 The Hudson's Bay Company builds another post on the Churchill River.

1690 Henry Kelsey begins his journey into present-day northern Manitoba from Hudson Bay to Saskatchewan River, near present-day The Pas.

1730s   French Canadian explorer La Vérendrye heads an expedition that builds outposts and forts and eventually explores the Red River and builds a fort near Lake Winnipeg.

1783   The Hudson's Bay Company builds Fort Churchill at the mouth of the Churchill River on the Hudson Bay.

1812   Thomas Douglas, fifth earl of Selkirk, a major investor in the Hudson's Bay Company, is granted a large tract of land in the Red River valley near Lake Winnipeg to settle Scottish immigrants.

1816   Red River Colony governor Robert Semple and nineteen colonists are killed in battle with Métis at Seven Oaks; Hudson's Bay Company allies capture and destroy the North West Company's Fort Gibraltar.

1821   Hudson's Bay and North West companies merge.

1849   Sayer trial in effect ends Hudson's Bay Company's fur trade monopoly.

1869   Canada agrees to purchase Rupert's Land from the Hudson's Bay Company; Louis Riel leads the Métis in opposition to Canadian annexation of Assiniboia, resulting in the Red River Rebellion and the establishment of a provisional government.

1870   The Métis convince the Canadian government to pass The Manitoba Act of 1870, making Manitoba a province, though only one-eighteenth its current size (dubbed the "Postage Stamp" province) and having a population of only about 12,000.

1881   Manitoba's borders are expanded westward and northward, increasing the size of the province five-fold and its population to 70,000.

1890   As a result of the Manitoba schools controversy, the dual education system is abolished and English is made the official language.

1900   As the world's demand for wheat grows, Manitoba begins a period of great prosperity.

1912   Manitoba's modern borders are established, tripling the province's area; the new northern section, up to the 60° line of latitude, gives Manitoba a coastline on the Hudson Bay as well as an expanded mining region.

1919   The Winnipeg General Strike in May follows from the soaring inflation and the labor discord after World War I.

1922   The United Farmers of Manitoba win control of the provincial government and retain power for more than three decades.

1956   Winnipeg elects its first non-Anglo-Saxon mayor, Stephen Juba, who was born in Canada of Ukrainian heritage; his popularity allows him to serve twenty-one consecutive years.

1984   The provincial government officially returns the French language to equal status with English.

1994   The Supreme Court of Canada grants the French-speaking citizens of Manitoba control over French-language education.

For Further Reading

Books

Pierre Berton, *The Last Spike: The Great Railway, 1881 to 1885*. New York: Doubleday, 2002. The prize-winning historian tells the story of Canada's first railroad, including the near-bankruptcy of the project, the land booms it triggered, and the Chinese workers who helped construct it.

Robert Craig Brown, *The Illustrated History of Canada*. Toronto: Key Porter Books Limited, 2000. With text from seven leading historians and helpful maps, illustrations, and other visual aids, this book takes the reader from Canada's earliest beginnings to the present day.

Gerhard John Ens, *Homeland to Hinterland: The Changing Worlds of the Red River Métis in the Nineteenth Century*. Toronto: University of Toronto, 1996. A detailed history of the Métis in Red River, including a discussion of the rebellion and their eventual general exodus from the province.

Don Gillmor, Achille Michaud, and Pierre Turgeon, *Canada: A People's History*, Volumes I and II. Toronto: McClelland and Stewart, 2001. A family reference book, these two texts cover the beginnings of Canada through the 1990s, discussing the wars, politics, empires, and settlers who affected the history of the land.

Roger E. Riendeau, *A Brief History of Canada*. Markham, Ontario: Fitzhenry and Whiteside, 2000. A survey of Canada from its earliest inhabitants to today, including many maps and illustrations.

Websites

The Province of Manitoba (www.gov.mb.ca). The provincial government's comprehensive site provides information on programs, parks, tourism, businesses, schools, and other topics.

The Hudson's Bay Company (www.hbc.com). Provides background on the company, including a useful overview of company history from its inception in 1670 through today.

The Centre for Rupert's Land Studies (www.uwinnipeg.ca). This University of Winnipeg site offers information and maps relevant to the human history of the huge territory owned by the Hudson's Bay Company from 1670 to 1870.

Works Consulted

Books

Pierre Berton, *The Promised Land.* Toronto: McClelland and Stewart, 1984. A noted historian describes the early immigration and settlement of the Canadian West.

Andrew R. Byers, ed., *Canada Coast to Coast.* Montreal: Reader's Digest Association (Canada), 1978. Describes places and things to see along Canada's main highways.

Gerald Friesen, *The Canadian Prairies: A History.* Lincoln: University of Nebraska Press, 1984. This comprehensive history of the western provinces focuses on politics, economics, and major historical events that shaped the west into the 1980s.

Marcel Giraud, trans. by George Woodcock, *The Métis in the Canadian West,* Volume I. London, England, and Lincoln, Nebraska: University of Alberta, 1986. Originally printed in 1945, this was the first scholarly examination of the Métis history.

Julia D. Harrison, *Métis.* Vancouver: Douglas and McIntyre, 1985. Harrison explores the mixed heritage and complicated history of the Métis of the Canadian West.

Andrew H. Malcolm, *The Canadians.* New York: St. Martin's Press, 1985. The author provides a general overview of Canada that seeks to understand the distinct characters of Canadians based on their backgrounds and regions.

Ronald A. Wells, ed., *Letters from a Young Emigrant in Manitoba.* Winnipeg: University of Manitoba, 1981. An interesting historical perspective.

George Woodcock, *The Hudson's Bay Company.* Toronto: Crowell-Collier, 1970. Woodcock explains the turbulent early years of the Hudson's Bay Company and its competitors, including the violence that led to its merger with the North West Company.

Internet Sources

Angelhair's Home Page. www.geocities.com.

Demographia. www.demographia.com.

Exchange District. www.exchangedistrict.org.

Manitoba Geobopological Survey. www.geobop.com.

North American Indigenous Games. www.zooznaig.com.

R.F. Morrison School. http://home.merlin.mb.ca.

Index

Picture Credits

About the Authors

Gordon D. Laws graduated with a Bachelor of Arts in English from Brigham Young University. He is the author of several short stories, numerous magazine articles, and the novel *My People*. Currently, he is a freelance writer and editor. Lauren M. Laws graduated with a Bachelor of Arts in history from Brigham Young University. She is a researcher and records expert. In addition to this work, Gordon and Lauren collaborated on *Exploring Canada: Alberta*. Gordon and Lauren live in Massachusetts with their son, Grant.

DATE